COMMUNITY LIBRARY
320 BENTON ST., VALLEY PARK, MO 63088

DATE DUE

COMMUNITY LIBRARY
320 BENTON ST., VALLEY PARK, MO 63088

IF THIS IS LOVE, WHY AM I SO LONELY?

IF THIS IS LOVE, WHY AM I SO LONELY?

Helene C. Parker, Ph.D.

with Doreen L. Virtue, Ph.D.

FAIRVIEW PRESS   *Minneapolis*

Published by Fairview Press, 2450 Riverside Avenue South, Minneapolis MN 55454.

Library of Congress Cataloging-in-Publication Data

Parker, Helene C., 1931–
    If this is love, why am I so lonely? / Helene C. Parker with Doreen L. Virtue.
        p.   cm.
    Includes index.
    ISBN 0-925190-82-9 (hc : alk. paper)
    1. Marriage. 2. Communication in marriage. 3. Man-woman relationships. 4. Self-realization. I. Virtue, Doreen L., 1958–   . II. Title.
HQ734.P189   1996
646.7'8—dc20   95-42847
                                                                    CIP

First Printing: January 1996

Printed in the United States of America
2000 99 98 97 96   7 6 5 4 3 2 1

Cover design: Circus Design

Publisher's Note: Fairview Press published books and other materials related to the subjects of family issues, relationships, and self-help. Its publications, including *If This Is Love, Why Am I So Lonely?* do not necessarily reflect the philosophy of Fairview Hospital and Healthcare Services or their treatment programs.

The paper used in this publication meets the minimum requirements of American National Standards for Information Sciences—Permanence of Paper for Printed Materials, ANSI Z329.48-1984.   ∞™

To those who have endured, suffered,
and lived the emotional pain of abusive relationships—
you have my compassion

To those who will read this book, and understand,
accept, and implement the tools and techniques—
you have my warranty, which is
the positive changes in your life.

To all of you who caused me emotional pain—thank you.
You have contributed to my success
in love, marriage, and career. Therefore
I am not lonely.

CONTENTS

ACKNOWLEDGMENTS

To those who left their mark on my emotional growth, both positive and negative. And to Doreen Virtue and Michael Tienharra, for their patience and gracious response to my wants in creating this book. I am grateful for the support of Fairview Press, and the skilled editing of Deborah Bihler.

Always . . .

To my husband, Ron, and our daughter, Lori, who have given me the negotiable, emotional environment that allows for the success of our family relationships (HELORON).

"If It Weren't for You, I'd Be Happy"

You opened this book for a reason. You are probably looking for solutions to the emotional pain in your life. Pain such as fear, doubt or depression. Perhaps you're dissatisfied with your current relationship. Or maybe you are single and tired of being alone.

Whatever the form of your emotional pain, pain is still pain, isn't it? Something in your life is causing the pain. Your life is different from the life you want. You want and even crave positive changes in your life.

In this book I will give you the same information that has helped thousands of my clients. These clients felt emotional pain similar to your own. You will learn the methods that have enabled my clients to attain the quality of life they have always wanted. Most of my clients take the information I give them, and use it to positively change their lives. Some balk at anything smacking of work or personal growth. As you read this book, you'll be making similar decisions. Will you decide to make the effort to positively change your life?

This book is the equivalent of a university course

1

that I call Emotional Education. It's like an advanced, graduate-level course designed to challenge and stimulate many of your preconceptions about relationships. Within this course, there is no right or wrong, good or bad—only healthy or unhealthy, functional or dysfunctional choices that affect your life. Choices that ultimately affect your love life, as well.

How Is the Love in Your Life?

Do you ever feel sad, upset, or lonely because you don't have the quality relationship you desire? Does it seem like you and your partner are strangers who don't really know one another? If so, you're not alone. Many people live their entire lives feeling unhappy about their relationships, unaware of the choices and options available to them.

What do you want in your relationship? What don't you want? What are you willing to do to get it? Are you willing to confront your partner? Are you willing to tell your partner what's wrong? Are you willing to tell your partner you don't want someone who lacks tenderness, or romance, or who is distant, aloof or verbally abusive?

Many people are told what they should want in a relationship, but don't follow their deepest desires to get what they really want. Instead, they perform or pretend.

When one partner withdraws or passively allows the other person to control everything, the controlling partner is in charge of the relationship, instead of both partners sharing equally. If not changed, this pattern leads to conflict.

Most people want a healthy, working relationship. They've either just left a relationship, they're just going into a new one, they are already in one, or they want one.

If people are truly honest with themselves, they will admit they want a relationship, but they also want free time, alone time, time with their friends, time to build their careers, and freedom to maintain their own schedule. What do you want? What's important to you?

Pleasing the other person is not the primary goal of a relationship, as you'll read throughout this book. The reason you feel unhappy in your relationship is because you're responding to behavior you do not like, and you either don't know how—or don't want—to challenge that destructive behavior.

If You Want to Make Positive Changes

This book is about making changes—changes that require commitment and effort on your part. The mere act of reading a self-help book cannot, in and of itself, miraculously change your life. But the information contained in this book can teach you ways to help yourself. All the tools you need are here. But you must put them to work yourself. This will not be an easy task, but the results will prove your efforts worthwhile!

Take Stephen and Barbara, for example. Stephen, a successful attorney forty-two years of age, felt exhausted after another evening of fighting with Barbara, his wife of six years. "That woman is never satisfied," he confided to his law partner. "I buy her almost anything she wants, and she still complains I don't do enough for her."

Across town, Barbara was also complaining to her best friend about her marriage. "Stephen never talks to me, and he never wants to spend any time together. He used to take me out all the time. We used to have so much fun together, but now all he does is work, work, work!" Barbara's eyes grew moist as she continued. "And another thing: we fight all the time. Last night, we even talked about getting a divorce."

Barbara's friend handed her my name and phone number. Stephen too, thought something had to be done, and agreed to accompany Barbara for therapy. The couple sat in my office their arms and legs crossed tightly. They took turns telling me their complaints. Stephen accused Barbara of being ungrateful for all his hard work and personal sacrifices. Barbara blamed Stephen's inattention for her lack of fulfillment.

Barbara looked at Stephen angrily and she began to stammer, "Why, if it weren't for you, I'd. . . ." At that point, I raised my hand and stopped her. I handed Barbara a small mirror and asked her to look at her own reflection.

"You were about to say to your husband, 'Why, if it weren't for you. . . .' I'd like to tell you to make the same statement to the person in the mirror." Both Barbara and Stephen looked at me with puzzled expressions.

My use of a mirror underscored what the couple needed to learn. Like most unhappy couples, Stephen and Barbara blamed one another for their own dissatisfaction. Stephen was unhappy because he had sacrificed hobbies and time for relaxation, and, had worked hard to buy Barbara the lifestyle she wanted.

Barbara felt unfulfilled because, instead of pursuing her own interests, she had spent her days cleaning the house and doting on her husband and three children. While careers and housework are both necessary parts of life, both spouses had gone overboard, sacrificing personal fulfillment. Both had expected marriage to be their sole source of happiness and contentment.

Like Barbara and Stephen, most discontented couples blame one another for their disappointments. Unless couples identify and understand the source of their problems, they can't solve them. Instead, they'll think, "If it weren't for you, I'd be happy."

It's no surprise that Barbara and Stephen are unhappy. Anyone who sacrifices his or her deepest personal interests is bound to feel frustrated and unfulfilled. Both partners in this marriage are running on empty, and expecting the other person to provide their emotional fuel.

When Giving Isn't Loving

It's better to give than to receive is a motto most of us heard in childhood. Many of our culture's values emphasize the importance and virtue of self-sacrifice. Sometimes, of course, putting another person's needs first is appropriate, such as fulfilling an infant's cries of hunger. But in adult love relationships, altruism usually backfires.

- Forty-two-year-old Mona overuses her credit cards buying gifts for her boyfriend, Brian. "I keep thinking he'll love me more, and we'll get closer to a commitment, if I shower him with presents," Mona explains.

- Thirty-three-year-old Stephanie resents her husband, Mark. "I want to exercise at the gym after work, but I have to fix supper and clean the house," she explains, clenching her teeth. Stephanie feels that Mark is preventing her from pursuing her fitness regimen.

- Twenty-eight-year-old Robert would like to join his company's softball team, but is certain his wife would complain. "The team practices and plays twice a week, and my wife gets really upset if I'm not home with her," he says.

If self-sacrifice were truly beneficial to a relationship, we would expect Mona, Stephanie, and Robert to have superb love lives. In fact, however, the reverse is true. All three are resentful because their personal needs aren't being fulfilled, and resentment oozes through a relationship like a deadly virus.

The Broken, Unspoken Agreement

Philosophers have long debated the existence of genuine altruism—giving without care for one's self. Many researchers believe that everyone gives, sacrifices, or helps for one reason only: the expectation of receiving a reward. The reward can consist of gratitude, fulfillment, a medal of honor, or admission into heaven. The expectation of reward is understandable and even honorable. But the point I'm making is that we don't give simply to give. We give because we want to give and we expect to be rewarded.

This type of thinking is carried into love relationships. "If I sacrifice for you," we think, "I expect you to always love me and make me happy in return." This expectation is always met with disappointment, however, and possibly devastation. The result of self-sacrifice is conflict, unfulfilled expectations and breakups.

"Look how much I do for you!" David screams at his wife, Lorraine. "I work at a lousy job I hate, just to afford the house *you* wanted." David feels trapped in an unful-filling profession, caught in a web of mortgage payments and a desire to keep his wife happy. What would David prefer to be doing? He dreams of starting his own man-ufacturing business—a desire that requires considerable start-up capitol. Deep down, David fears the immensity of his self-employment dream. It's easier for him to blame Lorraine.

Lorraine is caught in the same game of blame. She would like to return to college, earn her teaching certifi-cate, and get a job, but fears David would leave her if she spent evenings at night school.

A fulfilling, successful relationship is built around two people taking care of their personal needs, side by side. There is only one person who can know and pur-sue your human needs and desires, and there is only one person who can fulfill these desires. You!

Contrast Lorraine and David's relationship with that of another couple—two people who take individual responsibility for fulfilling their own needs. Connie and Anthony have been married fourteen years, and have two daughters, ten and twelve years old.

When they were first married, Connie stayed home to care for the house, and later the children. During that time, Connie maintained an active life with tennis, vol-unteer work, and long-term friendships. She went on overnight trips with her female friends, displayed her photographs at the county fair contest, took interesting adult education classes, and kept in shape at the gym. When asked if she sacrificed anything for the sake of her husband or children, Connie smiles and says "Of course not!"

When the girls got a little older, Connie decided to return to work outside the home. She knew her interests centered around artistic and creative endeavors, as well as working with other women. She opened a small photography studio specializing in glamour photos, and within a year was making a respectable profit.

Anthony is proud of Connie and happy to have such a vivacious wife. "Connie's so alive, so interested in her projects," he says. Like Connie, Anthony actively pursues his own personal interests, such as golfing and watching football with his friends. The couple also enjoys hobbies together, including nature walks and mountain climbing with the children.

The Virtue of Selfishness

We all have needs, interests, and values. They include:

- Time. This can be time alone, or with a loved one, friends, children, or family
- Play and hobbies, including sports, travel, collecting, reading—anything that gives us fulfillment
- The pursuit of money, prestige, career advancement, or validation
- Sex, romance, and attention from our mate

Most of us know what our needs and interests are; after all, we've had them for many years. So why should we expect these needs to disappear just because we fall in love or get married? In truth, these needs never leave us.

Couples newly in love sometimes put these needs on hold concentrating their attention on the new relationship. As the couple's commitment grows, do they continue, out of habit, to keep their personal interests at bay?

If they do, their self-sacrifice catches up to them. That's when blame enters the picture: "If it weren't for you, I'd be happy." The wife starts imagining how nice life would be if her husband wasn't around to interfere with her happiness. The husband dreams of the freedom he would feel without the constraints and shackles of his wife's expectations.

"But I can't be selfish!" protest the husband. But the question that should asked is, Which is more selfish: sacrificing your normal, human needs out of fear or insecurity, or taking care of your own needs and thus presenting your partner with a loving, fulfilled person?

What would you think of a woman who stopped eating, and then blamed her husband because she was hungry? Or a man who decided to forsake sleep, and then resented his wife because he was tired? We, alone, are responsible for fulfilling our individual physical needs. It's no different for our emotional and intellectual needs!

Do you recall how you felt, as a child, when you saw the adult who raised you in a bad mood? Perhaps your mother was upset because she had so much housework to do or your father was unhappy because he was mowing the lawn instead of playing golf. Did you feel anxious, guilty, or afraid?

Contrast those memories with the way you felt when your mother, father, or adult guardian was in a relaxed, happy mood. You likely felt warm, safe, and happy. The loving, responsible choice in any relationship—especially a love relationship—is to fulfill your own human needs and make yourself a happy, whole person.

After all, isn't that the kind of person with whom you'd want to be in a relationship?

First Me, Then Us

Most people desire a fulfilling relationship, one that feels safe, supportive, and loving. It's a natural, normal desire, and one worth pursuing. Unfortunately, problems arise when people get confused about *how* to achieve this desire.

After all, we receive no formal education about how to make a relationship work. We're left blind and alone, groping our way through the dark hallways of lessons about love. Sure, our parents, friends, and the media serve as examples of what a relationship is supposed to look like. But do they really have the qualities of the relationship we crave? Usually not. Most of us don't grow up in an environment that teaches us about healthy relationships.

Many dissatisfied couples seek professional help to resolve their differences. In the first session, the marriage counselor typically hears: It's all my wife's fault! or I should have married a different man. Why can't you just do things my way for once? My spouse just doesn't listen to me! In other words, both partners are completely focused on blaming difficulties on the other person.

Blame, however, serves no useful purpose in resolving relationship problems. In fact, blaming wastes time for both partners and the marriage counselor. Blaming implies someone was bad and deserves to be chastised or punished. But how could punishment bring a couple closer and bring back loving feelings? The answer, of course, is that couples who engage in blaming and punishing are dissatisfied and unfulfilled emotionally. Underneath all that blaming is a silent scream of emotional pain—a plea for love and understanding.

Anyone who feels emotionally hurt, misunderstood

or mistreated naturally becomes hostile and defensive, and is tempted to retaliate against the other person. But if the end goal is truly the same for both partners—to have a harmonious, loving relationship—there's no time to waste on blame, punishment, or retaliation.

All relationship problems are solvable in one way or another! Either the partners will work out a negotiated solution, or they will dissolve the relationship. Some couples will admit they are incompatible. It's not that one partner is wrong and the other is right, just that their goals and values are out of sync. The tools to achieve a loving partnership with yourself and others are all in this book. These tools were developed over years of studying and successfully treating people who were frustrated by unmet self-needs and wants for love and fulfillment.

Of course I'm not implying that every one of my clients had fairy tale endings. Through therapy, some decided to leave their relationships. But they were all successes, in the end, because the process of therapy made each more aware of the necessity of readying themselves for a future relationship. So instead of leaving one bad relationship and diving headfirst into another (an all-too-common pattern), each learned the choices and decisions necessary for success in a new relationship.

What these clients learned through hours and hours of therapy, first and foremost, was that all relationship successes and problems stem from one's self. This is not a version of blaming the victim, but rather a way of putting you in charge of your life. Many people feel helplessly out of control over their emotional lives, silently screaming, "How can I get the love that I want?" The answer: Only when you are ready to honestly assess what you are looking for, why you want it, and the actions you've taken in the past. You can only be ready for a successful, healthy relationship when you have a successful, healthy relationship with yourself.

The tools in this book are not quick-fix remedies. Beware of any person, book or tape that claims to have easy, painless answers to relationship problems! It takes effort, practice, and a willingness to confront and then change ingrained habits. Just reading a book won't produce miraculous solutions in a relationship, just as the mere act of reading a music book doesn't create a virtuoso. But learning to play the piano, and learning healthy relationship skills are both obtainable. Once learned, however, they must be practiced.

Sometimes people get frightened, frustrated, or discouraged by the amount of effort required to make positive changes in their lives. The rewards are worth the effort. Hang in there! You may be tempted to put the book down, as you read about the methods and tools for achieving and enhancing a relationship. This is a normal response.

Vicky, a forty-two year-old mother of two, married for ten years, is a perfect example. Vicky and her husband, Ben, entered therapy because their constant fighting had driven them to consider divorce. Vicky figured I would say that all their problems were Ben's fault, and then everything would be solved. But Vicky was shocked when I pointed out that her own behavior was contributing to the couple's problems. Furthermore, I gave Vicky homework assignments!

"At that point I decided marriage counseling was useless," Vicky remembers. "Looking back, however, I was just frightened at looking at myself. Dr. Parker's assignments were difficult with all the writing I had to do, but I really did learn a lot about myself. Therapy was a lot more work than I expected—sometimes it was even frightening—but it was definitely worth it. I'm so glad I didn't drop out. Now I know Ben and I will stay married, and our children will grow up with two loving parents."

Their children will also receive the greatest gift of all: learning, by example, how two healthy people contribute to a healthy, fulfilling love relationship. In that way, Vicky and Ben's children will be more apt to choose a healthy love partner and will be less likely to divorce.

First *Me,* Then *Us*

When you respect, know, and like yourself, you naturally feel at ease around others. Instead of guarding, hiding, or pretending, you are authentic and vulnerable with your partner.

Loneliness isn't merely cured by physical proximity to another person. Many people feel lonely, even though they live full-time with another person. Maybe you've had the experience of being at a crowded party and feeling all alone.

Existential philosophers argue that each of us, in truth, really is alone. Yet there is a perfectly healthy, perfectly natural, human craving to connect emotionally with another person. Loneliness comes from feeling disconnected with one's self. If you are uncomfortable with yourself, you won't feel comfortable around others. This means your partner isn't in love with or married to the true you, but to the false persona you present to your partner. How lonely!

You are a unique, multifaceted individual, a combination of your past experiences and individual goals, beliefs, and habits. These different human facets, called layers lie within you, all of them affecting the quality of your relationships. To reach the heart of your relationship patterns, these layers must be peeled off, one at a time—like peeling an onion. As we peel, a greater awareness of your own important needs, wants and desires come to light. The result is a dramatically increased self-understanding of our needs and wants, and what you should avoid in relationships.

Five Relationship Patterns that Never Work

Let's start the process by looking at past patterns in your relationships. A pattern is a similar set of circumstances that repeatedly shows up in your life. For example, Bonnie kept falling in love with men who abused alcohol or drugs. Lorraine had a series of relationships with hot-tempered and abusive men. Ron's girlfriends all cheated on him, and left him for other men. A cyclical pattern repeats itself over and over.

Relationship patterns can be subtle, as well. Teresa noticed this pattern in her ten-year marriage. "Every time I try to get emotionally close to Eric, he seems to pull away from me. I feel hurt by his distance, so I start ignoring him. That seems to make Eric insecure or something, because that's when he starts treating me really nicely. The only way I get attention from my husband is by pretending to ignore him!"

Unhealthy relationship patterns occur when we take

on a role instead of communicating our true feelings and opinions to our partner. Many of these roles are learned in childhood, and later carried into adult relationships. These roles include: Martyr/Victim, Rescuer, Placater, Enabler and Blamer. Sometimes, we unconsciously perform these roles instead of being authentic with a partner out of fear: fear of hurting someone's feelings; fear of saying something leading to a fight; fear of abandonment; or fear of rejection.

Yet the horrible irony is that our worst fears come true in relationships precisely because we choose to play roles rather than choose to be honest and authentic. At first, It may seem that these roles give us power and control in a relationship. But they don't give us the true power that would nurture us—self-esteem, emotional intimacy, and self-love.

You may already be aware of some of your own relationship patterns. You can investigate those patterns in greater detail by asking yourself the questions below. The best and most accurate answers to these types of questions are usually the first responses that come to mind.

Please answer "Often," "Sometimes," "Rarely," or "Never" to the following questions about how you act, feel, and think within your love relationships.

1. Do I feel my partner is the cause of most relationship problems?
2. Do I feel unappreciated by my relationship partners?
3. Do I give, and get nothing in return?
4. Do I act submissive to avoid conflicts?
5. Do I feel like a second-class citizen in my relationships?

6. Do I feel it is risky for me to express my opinion to my partner?
7. Do I fear my partner is going to reject or abandon me?
8. Do I feel more like a silent partner, than an equal partner, in my relationships?
9. Do I end up taking care of (mothering or fathering) my partner?
10. Do I have to watch out for my partner's well-being?
11. Do I feel pressured to fix my partner's problems?
12. Do I feel powerful because I know my partner needs me so much?
13. Does my advice to my partner seem to fall on deaf ears?
14. Do I find myself bailing my partner out of jams?
15. Do I fall in love with people who are in dire circumstances?
16. Do I attract needy people?
17. Do I put my own needs second to the needs of my partner?
18. Do I give up my free time to do things that please my partner?
19. Do I see myself as less important than my partner?
20. Do I tend to clam up, or downplay my intelligence, to avoid intimidating or threatening my partner?
21. Do I put myself down in an effort to make my partner feel better?
22. Do I "stuff" my feelings, rather than express them?
23. Do I smile and pretend to act happy around my partner, when inside I'm boiling with anger?

24. Do I give my partner insincere compliments and flattery to receive his or her gratitude, or to avoid conflict?
25. Do I forgive my partner's unsuitable behavior too quickly?
26. Do I cover up or excuse my partner's inappropriate behavior to other people?
27. Do I help my partner rationalize his or her errant behavior?
28. Do I encourage my partner to engage in risky behavior, because I know that's really what my partner wants to do?
29. Do I call in sick to my partner's employer, to cover up my partner's absenteeism?
30. Do I get involved with people addicted to drugs, alcohol, or other compulsive behavior?
31. Do I blame myself for my partner's improper or rude behavior?
32. Do I think my partner would act differently if only I could improve the way I act or look? Do I say yes when I really mean no?
33. Do I believe my partner is at fault for 99 percent of the problems in our relationship?
34. Would my life be a lot better if my partner didn't act like a loser so much of the time?
35. Do I think my partner tries to blame me for things that are really all his or her fault?
36. Do I believe that every time our relationship begins to improve my partner messes it up again?
37. Do I feel frustrated because my partner won't take my advice about how to fix l his or her faults?
38. Do I feel angry because my partner says and does things deliberately to get me upset?

39. Do I think my partner goes out of his or her way to create problems in our relationship?
40. Do I think my partner needs help to fix his or her problem(s), so we can get on with our lives?

Interpreting Your Answers

The patterns that have interfered with your past or present relationships will surface as you look through the interpretations below. This quiz provides valuable information for breaking unhealthy, unfulfilling relationship patterns. Keep in mind, while scoring your quiz, that there are no right or wrong answers—this isn't a quiz that you pass or fail, but a quiz that gives insight into your relationship patterns. In that respect, failure happens only when a person fails to identify unhealthy relationship patterns!

In the descriptions of each role, notice that no one is implying anyone is a bad person. These are roles people adopt hoping to get more power, control, harmony, or love. In other words, their intentions may be positive. But playing these roles yields only negative results: loneliness, chaos, dishonesty, distrust. Think of the roles as a costume you may have donned at one time. You are not the role, you have performed the role. You can remove the costume and choose never to don it again.

Scoring your answers
Often = 3 points
Sometimes = 2 points
Rarely = 1 point answer
Never = 0 points

Total your totals for questions 1 through 8.

14–24 points. You actively engage in the role of Martyr/Victim. You frequently feel like the underdog—someone mistreated and used by others. You aren't quite ready, however, to admit your own responsibility in accepting the Martyr/Victim role. You may even enjoy some of the attention and pity you receive from other people who view you as a long-suffering, saintly type. The Martyr/Victim may appear to be powerless, but in reality holds a lot of power and control in the relationship—the Martyr/Victim is a master at wielding guilt. The bottom line remains the same, however: it doesn't feel good nor is it fulfilling to be a Martyr/Victim. It's actually a very lonely role. After all, when you are less than or greater than your love partner, how can emotional intimacy occur? How can you connect?

0–13 points. There are three possibilities: you have adopted the role of Martyr/Victim in past relationships; you use it infrequently in your present relationship; or, in answering the questions, you downplayed how often you use the Martyr/Victim role. Either way, your Martyr/Victim tendencies are one reason you feel lonely, frustrated, or unfulfilled in your love life.

Total your points for questions 9 through 16.

14–24 points. You have adopted the role of Rescuer as a regular pattern in your relationships. You find yourself attracting a variety of people who need rescuing, such as the unemployed, addicted, and physically or mentally ill. Much of your time, energy and even money is spent helping others. But there's a catch, because your rescue work isn't really philanthropic or charitable, is it?

In truth, you feel elevated by the power of being the Rescuer, feeling superior to those who need your help. As much as it bothers you to be around helpless people, it does give you satisfaction to know you're needed. You feel smart, successful, and wise around the underlings who look up to you or who rely on you. You only get upset when they shun your advice, or don't express appreciation.

But the price you pay for adopting the Rescuer role is high because there's no level playing field between you and your partner, there's no true emotional connection. There's a gap filled only with loneliness caused by hidden agendas and dishonesty. In a relationship, a Rescuer acts more like a parent than an equal partner. The parenting role inherently creates distance between the two partners, preventing the closeness and mutual respect necessary for deep, emotional fulfillment and the elimination of loneliness.

There is also continuous turmoil because it's impossible to control your partner's behavior. Wouldn't it be a relief to relax with a partner and not worry about taking care of him or her?

0–13 points. You have adopted the Rescuer role on occasion, and are drawn to the power it seems to give you. Yet the role isn't completely satisfying so you use it infrequently. Deep down you probably realize, that the Rescuer role will not result in the fulfillment you desire. It's a bandage covering the real problems in the relationship. Are you ready to shed this role for something really honest and rewarding?

Total your points for questions 17 through 24.

14–24 points. You go out of your way to avoid conflict, and have adopted the role of Placater as your way
of maintaining peace and tranquillity in the relationship.
Like the other roles, the Placater role is a way of hiding
your true feelings and opinions, so it interferes with honest emotional intimacy. The term, Placater, is similar to
the term, Play Actor, both in sound and in definition.
The Placater gives compliments, flattery, and praise to
manipulate another person's behavior. The core of the
Placater role is a desire for power and control in the relationship. In essence, the Placater says, " I want you to
behave in certain ways, in exchange for my being nice
to you." Placaters fear emotional closeness, a fear borne
in the "you wouldn't love me if you knew the real me"
belief.

0–13 points. You adopt the Placater role occasionally when you want more power in the relationship, or
when you fear conflict or rejection. You vacillate
between an intense desire for emotional connection with
your partner, and fears of conflict or abandonment. The
only trouble, as you already know, is that when you play
the Placater role you are intensely lonely!

Total your points for questions 25 through 32.

14–24 points. You employ the role of the Enabler,
and may not be aware of it. The Enabler, like some of
the other roles, has intense fears of conflict, rejection,
and abandonment. Instead of confronting a partner for
unsuitable behavior, the Enabler ignores it. Enablers
even blame themselves for the behavior of their partner.
For example, "I know he wouldn't drink so much if I lost
some weight." Enablers are masters at keeping their

22

heads in the sand and pretending to themselves and others that everything's perfect. They rationalize, distort, and deny any problems in their relationships. The only trouble is: Enablers are extremely unhappy, frustrated, and lonely. They suffer from low self-esteem, and their Enabling behavior only ensures that their self-esteem will continuously erode.

Furthermore, the pattern of self-blame does no good because Enablers are not ready to admit responsibility for choosing an unhealthy partner or continuing in a dysfunctional relationship. Claiming responsibility for past behavior is the only road out of Enabling behavior and dysfunctional relationships. Taking responsibility puts you in charge and gives you the power you crave— simply by saying, "I was in control when I chose this relationship; now I have just as much power to stop or change this relationship."

0–13 points. You occasionally adopt the role of the Enabler or downplayed your answers because you fear admitting how much you employ it. Perhaps you once acted the role of a full-time Enabler, but educated yourself about its destructiveness. Like the others, this role is just as destructive in small doses as it is in large doses. In a truly healthy—and therefore truly fulfilling—relationship, there are no needs for any roles at all. Why not go all the way, and shed the Enabler role altogether?

Total your points for questions 33 through 40.

14–21 points. You have adopted the role of Blamer. The Blamer points the finger of fault at others, and really believes there would be no problem if everyone else would just change. The trouble is: no one takes your advice, do they? Underneath the Blamer's behavior is a deep-seated fear of being criticized or rejected. If someone begins to blame the Blamer for a problem, the response is fear or anger. Blamers become defensive, and aggressively deny any wrongdoing.

Blamers also have an all-or-nothing viewpoint about blame and fault, believing others are always at fault. They are unwilling to consider the possibility of shared responsibility in relationship problems, *or* solutions. Blamers are so wary of being blamed, that they overcompensate by aggressively blaming others. It helps Blamers when they understand that no one is saying they are entirely at fault for their love-life difficulties. The issues of fault and blame are irrelevant when it comes to solving relationship problems! It serves no useful purpose to label anyone "right" or "wrong." The only productive labeling is the classification of healthy or unhealthy behavior. Then, instead of blaming someone for unhealthy behavior, we work to change it into healthy behavior.

0–13 points. Is there a possibility you downplayed your answers because you wanted to be seen in a favorable light? Blamers cannot stand anything smacking of criticism. To a Blamer, everything is about winning and losing. If you feel blamed, you feel you've lost a contest or battle. Yet Blamers ultimately lose because this unhealthy behavior blocks· emotional connection and intimacy. People who successfully shed the role of Blamer are those people who see the light, so to speak, that relationships are not about wins and losses. It's a love relationship, not a baseball game! Relationships are about partnership, shared responsibility, and mutual growth.

Pattern Cycles

Did you recognize yourself or your partner in any of those roles? If you did, you have taken an important step toward having the fulfilling relationship you want.

Not everyone plays only one of these roles; sometimes people use more than one role, and your quiz answers may reflect this tendency. Most relationship problems do stem from a partner adopting a combination of the Martyr/Victim, Rescuer, Placater, Enabler, and Blamer roles. For example, Kevin and Dawn would alternate different roles, as if by a mutually understood agreement. Here is the couple's pattern when they came in for marriage counseling:

> *First.* Dawn acted as a Martyr/Victim. She was exhausting herself by trying to be perfect in all areas of her life. Not only did Dawn hold a full-time managerial position, but she also insisted on keeping her large house spotless around the clock. Dawn epitomized a superwoman, but didn't see it as her own choice. Instead, she complained of being a victim of Kevin's pressures to be perfect.

> *Second.* Kevin would Enable Dawn's anger by walking on eggshells in her presence. Instead of confronting Dawn for choosing to live in "super-woman hell," Kevin would try to please her and stay out of her way. Kevin felt uncomfortable being home whenever Dawn was in a cleaning frenzy. So he'd leave.

> *Third.* Dawn saw Kevin's behavior as an avoid-

ance of his responsibilities. She Blamed him for the unhappiness and despair she felt. It got to the point where Dawn blamed Kevin for most of the problems in her life. She continuously complained to Kevin about her unhappiness and his shortcomings.

Fourth. To appease Dawn, Kevin would Placate her and agree to whatever she said. He wanted to be honest with her about his feelings, but Kevin feared incurring even more of Dawn's wrath. So he Placated her.

Fifth. Kevin finally got fed up with the tension and anger in his household. But instead of confronting Dawn, he decided to Rescue her. Although the couple was struggling to pay their bills, Kevin convinced Dawn to quit her job so she'd have more free time.

Both Dawn and Kevin were amazed to find that even after Dawn stopped working, their quarrels only worsened! It took months of hard work in therapy before the couple admitted that Dawn's job and the housework were just symbols and symptoms of the true underlying problem in their relationship: a lack of honesty between them, and a lack of personal responsibility for meeting their own needs.

Dawn learned to pace herself, and, with Kevin's help, keep a neat house and also hold a part-time job. Now she has free time for herself. Kevin learned to be more forthright with his wife, instead of pretending nothing was wrong.

The roles Dawn and Kevin had adopted were

unhealthy and dysfunctional. Dysfunctional roles lead to dysfunctional relationships.

WHAT DO YOU WANT?

When a couple comes in for marriage counseling, the partners know one thing for certain: they are not happy. Dissatisfied partners usually analyze, obsess, and continually contemplate their unhappiness.

This doesn't resolve anything, however, because the focus needs to be on something so seemingly simple that most people miss it. They each need to ask , "What do I want?"

Here's a common complaint I'll hear from couples in therapy: "Dr. Parker, I don't know what's wrong. I'm just so miserable in my marriage."

People usually go to great lengths to develop theories and reasons to explain their misery. Maybe they'll watch a talk show about marital problems, or read a magazine article and they'll say, "That's it! That's the problem with my marriage just like that person on television!" Then they'll run out and buy the self-help manual being plugged on the talk show, and try to diagnose the basis of their problem themselves. The cycle is exhausting just to think about, and such a waste of time and effort.

I cut through all that garbage by asking my clients one simple question: "If you're not happy with what you've got, what exactly do you want instead?" Few people are prepared to hear such a question, let alone to answer it. While many people grapple with thoughts like, "I'm so unhappy," few people take the time to consider, "Well, what would make me happy?" "What can I do to make myself happy?" They don't realize they have the irrefutable right to contest, and change, their current life conditions.

So let me ask you the same question: "What exactly do you want?"

Needs and Wants

Before we delve further into answering that question, let's look at the basic difference between needs and wants. I've found a lot of needless suffering is based on confusing a *need* with a *want*.

There are distinct differences between needs and wants. A need is a necessity for physical and spiritual survival. There are two types of needs: physical and spiritual.

Physical needs include
- food
- air
- water
- shelter
- adequate clothing

Spiritual needs include

- self nurturing
- happiness
- spiritual fulfillment
- peace of mind

In other words, needs are food for the body and for the soul. If our needs are not met, it is a disaster! Our physical and mental health seriously suffers; we may die physically or spiritually if our needs go unmet. We have no choice but to seek food, water, air and shelter. Self nurturing is also a need, because it is a non-optional necessity. Self nurturing—call it contentment, or spirituality if you like—is vital to mental health, and a necessary ingredient of self-love and love for others.

When both the physical and the spiritual needs are self-met, you are well on your way to self-actualization. Your needs are your responsibility. Only you can fulfill your needs. This enables the self to have power. To give this power away—by expecting someone else to provide for your needs—is the difference between being independent versus dependent. Independent adults take care of themselves. Dependent adult display the emotional age of a child. As dependent adults we are neither happy nor fulfilled, we actually *give away* our happiness when we expect another person to provide for our needs.

A want, on the other hand, is a strong desire or preference that enhances our needs. If wants are unfulfilled, we are disappointed, sad or angry but we won't die. When people are unhappy in relationships, it is usually because of unmet wants. And they are frequently unaware of what those unmet wants or expectations are. Unless we know what we want, we can't ask for or get it.

The difference between needs and wants

Needs	Wants
Necessary for physical and mental survival. Non-optional.	Strong desires or preferences that enhance our needs. Optional.

Wants fall into two general categories: Relationship Wants—those that involve another person; and Personal Wants—things that just involve ourselves.

Relationship wants include

- romance
- love
- understanding
- sex
- companionship
- emotional support
- caring
- financial security
- intimacy
- trust
- honesty
- feeling safe

Personal wants include

- relaxing
- fun

- alone time
- achievements
- personal possessions beyond our basic survival needs

Sometimes people mistake deprivation for devotion. "I'm sacrificing fun, relaxation, and hobbies for you," the partner thinks, "so you'd better make me happy in return, or I'll punish you by abandoning or fighting with you." People who hold this belief will expect their partner to fulfill their personal wants. No one but you can fulfill your personal wants. I cannot emphasize this strongly enough! This one issue is the source of the majority of personal and relationship dissatisfaction.

If you don't take care of your own wants (for free time, leisure time, or alone time), those wants will be unmet. The result? You will be dissatisfied.

If this sounds simple, it's because it is simple!

Yet I've found so many people overlook this crucial core of personal and relationship happiness. Everyone seems to overcomplicate relationship problems by looking for complex explanations for their dissatisfaction. Yet the core of most relationship problems is simple: unmet wants. Once my clients are taught the importance of fulfilling their own personal wants, the strife and tension in their relationships almost immediately eases.

I teach my therapy clients to speak in terms of their wants, but also to know that they may not always get these wants fulfilled. For example, a woman may say to her husband, "I want you to go shopping with me." If her husband says, "No, but thanks for asking," the woman's want goes unfulfilled. But if she hadn't asked, there was little possibility of her want being met. At least, by asking, fulfillment becomes possible!

No one should be reprimanded for expressing their wants. You are responsible for communicating your want, and your partner is responsible for communicating his or her reaction to your want.

Babies naturally vocalize their wants, crying loudly when they are hungry, thirsty, or cold. As children, we learn to squelch this natural expression of our wants. A child asks her aunt for a cookie, and is reprimanded by her mother with a firm, "That's not polite to ask!" So the child stops asking for what she wants, and wonders why she feels frustrated.

THE VIRTUES OF
SELFISHNESS

"But I can't be selfish!"—this is the response I hear most often when I explain the importance of fulfilling one's own wants. Many frustrated couples enter therapy because of unmet wants. The husband blames the wife, and the wife blames the husband. There's a reluctancy to say, "It's my own fault if my wants are unfulfilled." This fear of appearing selfish keeps us from meeting our own wants, having fun or being good to ourselves.

Selfishness is commonly confused with self-centeredness. Taking care of one's self—selfishness—is vital to personal and relationship health. If we, ourselves, meet our needs and wants, we are happy and content. If we are happy and content, we naturally have a positive effect on the relationship. This is called positive selfishness. The warmth and glow radiating from contented partners creates the setting for a warm, emotionally fulfilling relationship.

Contrast that image of two content partners with another picture: two tense, unfulfilled, and resentful partners. Striking, isn't it? Almost like comparing a warm, spring day with a freezing cold winter day. Which atmosphere would you like to live in? Which picture feels most conducive to the growth of the partners and the relationship?

Only one person can control getting your needs met: you. Your wants are met through negotiation, either with yourself ("What steps do I need to take to get what I want?") or with others ("Let's discuss how we can both get what we want, by working together."). It's called "self-responsibility" and it carries big rewards—high self-esteem, self power, and self-control.

No one else is responsible for your needs, and no one else can give you permission to fulfill your needs. Conversely, no one can deny you your needs, unless you *let* them.

This doesn't mean you can always fulfill your wants if isolated from other people. Many wants, such as romance and sex, require the cooperation of other people. These wants are achieved through negotiation, in the manner discussed throughout this book.

Selfishness versus Self-Centeredness

Positive selfishness builds self-esteem and healthy relationships. Self-centeredness, in contrast, destroys relationships. Self-centeredness is a toxic behavior rooted in a desire to control and manipulate others. Its foundation is fear, insecurity, and a defensive desire to protect one's self. Its result is the loss of self power.

People sometimes say, "If you're meeting your own

Selfishness says:	**Self-Centeredness says:**
"I am only in control of my own self."	"I want to control you."
"I take care of fulfilling my wants."	"I expect you to know what I want."
"Our mutual love is dependent on both of us having high self-esteem."	"I will manipulate you to fulfill me."
"We are two satisfied individuals, taking care of our own wants, side by side."	"When you become confident, I feel afraid that you'll leave me."
"I support your efforts to fulfill your own wants."	"If you loved me, you'd put my wants ahead of your own."
"I don't expect you to read my mind. I'll tell you what I want in our relationship, and negotiate when necessary."	"Look at how I've sacrificed for you."
	"A loving partner would automatically know what I want, without my having to say anything. If you really loved me, you'd take responsibility for giving me what I need and want."

needs, you're a selfish person." To which I reply, "Of course! Who else can meet your needs?" Meeting your own needs is both healthy and natural. If you think about it, when you take care of your own needs and express your wants, you are actually giving your partner a gift! They are receiving the gift of a contented, relaxed, and emotionally available person.

So let's not interchange the words *selfish* and *self-centeredness* any longer. They have opposite meanings. Selfishness means, "I am in control of myself," while self-centeredness means, "I want to manipulate you to meet my needs and wants."

Self-centeredness stems from a desire to control others. A common outcome of self-centeredness is The Martyr Syndrome. This occurs when a person doesn't pursue happiness, then blames others for the resulting unhappiness. The Martyr tries to elicit guilt from others in order to feel in control, needed, and loved. Unfortunately, Martyr Syndrome behavior never results in good feelings or positive love.

For example, Fred felt resentment toward his wife, Bianca. "I work fifty and sixty hour weeks, but Bianca doesn't appreciate how hard I work," he complained. Fred blamed Bianca for his misery, and reminded her about it around the clock. He'd grumble every night when he opened the bills, and tell Bianca, "Aren't you lucky to have a husband who works so hard to support you?" While watching television together, a commercial about golf or bowling would trigger resentful and aggressive comments from Fred like, "If only I didn't have to work so much . . ."

During the counseling session, Fred and I identified his unfulfilled wants. Clearly, Fred's want of time for leisure and play wasn't being met. But was this really Bianca's fault? Of course not. We worked on getting Fred more organized at work, so he could be more productive, and work fewer hours. (It turned out Fred was wasting quite a bit of time at work grumbling to his co-workers around the water cooler, or on the telephone).

Then we worked on Fred's beliefs about leisure time. While he craved having more free time to relax and play, Fred struggled with fears that playing is unproductive and wasteful. Fred was afraid to play—an attitude he'd adopted from his workaholic father (who probably had struggled with the Martyr Syndrome himself). Instead, Fred blamed his wife for his reluctance to take care of his own wants.

Once Fred learned it was not only okay for him to go golfing—but actually a necessity—he blossomed into another person. His facial expression relaxed, he lost weight, and his relationship with himself and with Bianca dramatically improved. All because Fred took charge of getting his basic human want for free time met!

Because the Martyr Syndrome is so common, let's look at another example. This case involves Valerie and Don. Their story may sound similar to that of someone you know.

As newlyweds, Valerie and Don were on a tight budget; it made sense for Valerie to pinch pennies on every purchase. But now—fifteen years later—the couple earns a comfortable income and are more than financially secure. But Valerie still acts like a pauper when it comes to buying necessities for herself.

She indulges her children and Don with name brand shoes, and then spends only two or three dollars on her own shoes—on sale, of course. Her family wears brand-new undergarments, but Valerie wears hers until they're hopelessly irreparable.

This bravado behavior is unnecessary and destructive. If you ask Valerie, she'll tell you she's sacrificing for the good of the family. What she is really doing, however, is trying to boost her self-esteem by a demonstration of suffering and sacrifice. She is a Martyr. Her good intentions are misguided. Her family's income is not dependent on her purchase of three dollar rather than sixty-five dollar shoes. On the other hand, Valerie's self-esteem is dependent on her meeting her own needs. When she wears uncomfortable or inappropriate shoes and clothing, her needs for decent clothing aren't being met. And as we've seen, our self-esteem is contingent upon being self responsible for our own needs and wants.

CONFUSING NEEDS WITH WANTS

A **need** is a necessity for survival, while a want is a life enhancer. Many times, we'll say we need something. But we don't actually *need* that object of our desire, because we'll survive without it. We want it, we don't need it.

Linda, a thirty-nine-year-old marketing director, says she needs a man, and she needs a relationship. Of course, Linda can survive without either. She's confusing a need with a want. This is not just an exercise in semantics, though. Because Linda believes she needs—and therefore must have—a man and a relationship, she acts needy. To be precise, we could label Linda's behavior as "wanty."

In relationships, Linda acts desperate—much like people act when their needs for air, food, water are unavailable. Think of a drowning woman gasping for air, and you get a picture of Linda's behavior in relationships. She becomes clingy, continuously asking her partner for reassurance.

Nobody wants to be in a relationship with a desperate, clingy person; it's impossible to love someone who shows so little regard for herself. Yet, because Linda confuses a need with a want, her behavior reflects her belief that she cannot survive without a relationship. Her needy behavior actually pushes away the very thing she wants most.

Wants and needs are confused in another way. Sometimes, people think of self-nurturing as an optional activity. They mistakenly believe that self-nurturing is a want. Yet, without self-nurturing activities, we feel empty and discontented. We must take care of ourselves first!

Self-nurturing is a real need, both physically and spiritually. Anything that brings you serenity, contentment, and peace of mind—whether listening to music, taking a walk, or playing with a pet—is your perfect right. You not only have the right to take care of yourself, you have the responsibility.

As we've already discussed, without self-love there can be no relationship love. You cannot truly love people who do not love themselves enough to take care of themselves. And you cannot love another person until you first give yourself the love you need.

Relationship Addictions

Some people believe, "I'm nothing without my wants. I must have this job, this car, a house in this neighborhood." Of course, we all have preferences and there is nothing wrong with desiring a beautiful home, a fancy car, or a fulfilling career. The trouble comes when our confusion of needs with wants leads to desperate pleas like: "I will just die if I don't get that job!" Or, "If my partner breaks up with me, or cheats on me, my life will be ruined!"

This fear-based thinking about relationships is codependency. Codependency comes from neediness, where needs are confused with wants. It leads to a relationship addiction. Someone once defined an addiction as "the out-of-control and aimless search for wholeness, happiness, and peace, through a relationship with a person, place, object, or event in order to produce a mood change." This is the core of codependency.

The relationship addict, or codependent, depends on their addictive process to avoid facing reality. The person who says, "I can't survive without a relationship," shows classic signs of addiction, including cravings, obsessions, tolerance, and withdrawal. Here are some signs of relationship addictions:

- feelings of desperation and urgency ("I must have a relationship right now!")
- fear of being alone ("I need to be with another person.")
- self-denigrating thoughts ("No one wants me, so I must be unlovable.")
- obsessive brooding over a past lover ("Should I call him? Should I, should I?")
- recklessly choosing a relationship partner ("Well, he's not perfect that's for sure. But it's better to be with him, than to be alone!")
- the continuous planning or mental rehearsal of how to get one's "love fix" met. ("Maybe I'll call Sue. No, I think I'll go to that singles bar. No, it would be better to go to Kevin's party and see which women show up.")

- Outrageous, or even dangerous, steps to find a relationship. ("I know it's unsafe to be out alone late at night. But how else am I going to meet someone unless I go to the popular singles' bars?") This is putting one's self in a dangerous environment, as portrayed in the movie *Looking for Mr. Goodbar.*
- Placement of oneself in financial jeopardy to achieve a relationship fix. ("I really need to save this money to pay my taxes, but I need to impress Sarah by taking her away for the weekend." Or: "I really need that dress so he will think I am sexually attractive.")

Relationship addicts believe they are in control of their mood changes, and the means to that mood change—a man, a woman, a relationship, sex—is what gives them that mood. The love addict chases after the high, or the thrill. But along with those highs come deep lows. Like a drug addict, the relationship addict accepts the lows to get the highs. But, the price for the highs is usually abusive behavior by the relationship partner.

Cynthia and Chester regularly scream, shout and hurl insults at one another. One time, they even got into a violent slugging match! After each fight, the couple would have passionate—almost desperate—sexual intercourse. Both Cynthia and Chester are addicted to the thrill and what they call excitement from the turmoil and drama of their relationship. They are addicted to their own soap opera, and fear that anything less than their high-drama lifestyle would be terminally boring.

Sometimes, the addiction is to the romantic gestures that come out of an unhealthy relationship. For example, Sylvia's boyfriend, George, showered her with expensive gifts of jewelry and clothing. However, George would also shower Sylvia with physical and verbal abuse. But Sylvia tolerated George's horrendous abuses because she was so hooked on the gifts. Sylvia would focus on George's apologies, accompanied by another opulent gift, and would believe him when he'd say, "I'll never do it again."

Relationship addicts' lives are completely centered around the fulfillment of their addiction. Every waking moment is spent planning, preparing, remembering, and getting their "love fix."

Of course, it's not true love that they are after, or that they are getting. Most relationship addicts have not had a real love relationship—with themselves or with another person—to compare with a false, or addictive, love relationship.

Relationship addiction, like all addictions, is based in self-shame and a sense of inadequacy. The love addict secretly believes he or she is inferior to others, or is defective, and guards this secret as if life depended upon it. Of course, most people can spot low self-esteem from a million miles away, which is why the relationship addict attracts their perfect match: someone else with low self-esteem. A person with high self-esteem is never attracted to someone with low self-esteem, at least not for long.

The two love addicts, with low self-esteem, play off of each other in an unspoken agreement to support one another's unhealthy relationship expectations. Thus, the woman who believes that all men abandon her will always find an abandoning man. The man who believes all women are irresponsible will have no trouble attracting an immature self-centered female. Healthy people don't waste their time—nor are they attracted to—dysfunctional love partners.

Those who want a healthy relationship, both with themselves and with a love partner, are those who

1. know what they want, and know the difference between needs and wants
2. know they are solely responsible for meeting their needs and wants
3. know the difference between behavior that is destructive—self-centered, abusive, controlling— and behavior that is constructive and healthy
4. ask themselves the question: "What's the price I must pay to get this prize? Do I have the self-control necessary to obtain this want? What steps must I take to get this want fulfilled?"

When we clarify within ourselves that we want a great relationship, but don't need one in order to survive—we detach and relax. This letting go attitude actually allows us to be ourselves in a relationship, rather than feeling a desperate need to pretend, "or else my partner won't like me." We can focus on our own behavior rather than reacting to cues from a partner. We become authentic.

It's ironic, when we let go and stop thinking a relationship is a do or die need, we relax and automatically become more lovable and attractive. No healthy person is attracted to a bottomless pit, which is the essence of a needy, codependent person. But a person who is content, happy, and self-loving is irresistible!

Appreciation Wants

Our desire to feel loved, wanted and appreciated—basic relationship wants—is one reason we enter into a relationship. It feels good when these relationship wants are met. Who doesn't want to feel loved and appreciated? However, men and women differ in the way they want love and appreciation expressed. For example, women deeply want to be cherished and adored. Men have strong desires for admiration and respect. These gender-related differences, if not understood and practiced, can lead to unnecessary relationship misunderstandings and blaming. The table on page 48 illustrates how men and women differ in their appreciation wants.

When we understand these gender-based differences, we have more empathy with our partners. For example, a man might feel hurt because he perceives his wife as being unloving when she corrects him in public. "She does it on purpose!" he fumes to himself.

But the wife, not realizing that she's emotionally stepping on her husband's ego, believes she's helping her husband. "I'm teaching him the correct way to say something; it is my way of expressing my love for him." I want to show him he married a smart woman who shares her expertise. Furthermore, the wife might experience her own emotional pain, believing her husband doesn't appreciate her. "He doesn't think I'm smart enough to give him advice," she might silently think. "He should compliment me for my intelligence more often."

If this couple could interpret one another's behavior through each other's eyes, both partners would drop some of their defensiveness. Instead of assuming that the other person is attacking, it would be apparent that the partner is just unaware. Instead of becoming distant and cold, or provoking a fight, the couple would calmly tell one another, "This is how I perceived your action, and this is why I didn't like it. I would appreciate it if you would, instead (not correct me in public; compliment me about my intelligence; not flirt with other people, and so on).”

He wants appreciation in this way	She wants appreciation in this way
“My partner asks for, and respects my advice.”	“My partner tells me I am special.”
“My partner treats me with courtesy and respect when we are alone, and when we are in public.”	“My partner keeps his word.”
	“My partner cares about my wants.”
“My partner doesn’t correct me in public.”	“My partner asks me to spend the rest of my life with him.”
“My partner compliments me for my skills and knowledge.”	
	“My partner doesn’t look at other women; he tells me I’m more beautiful than other women.”
“My partner tells me she is proud of me.”	
	“My partner listens to me when I’m talking.”

Wantiness and Neediness

Another great source of unhappiness in a relationship is not knowing what you want, and confusing a want with a need. True independence comes from taking charge—choosing what you want, and then taking responsibility for getting those wants met.

In healthy, functional families, children are taught the difference between needs and wants. Functional parents are nurturers, who teach their children to take responsibility for getting their own needs and wants met. Rather than perpetually rescuing the child, functional parents teach independence, responsibility, and maturity.

Children who grow up in dysfunctional families usually miss the opportunity to learn this important lesson. They grow up feeling that something is missing from their lives, and that they should find another person to fill in the missing pieces. Such a person goes from one unsatisfying relationship to another, believing that the right love partner will fill the void in their soul. But, these people are continually disappointed in their love relationships. Expecting others to take care of our needs and wants inevitably leads to frustration and anger. The responsibility is yours.

Desperate and needy people are also vulnerable to the singles scene, where they attract equally emotionally unhealthy people. Philip complained that every woman he met was helpless. "My last girlfriend was on the brink of bankruptcy when I met her," he says. "If I hadn't helped her get a job, she would've lost her house and her car. Our entire relationship became wrapped around what I could do to save her from herself, and she never even thanked me! I would just like to meet a woman who has her act together."

Rescuing is another by-product of growing up in a dysfunctional family and not learning early on to take care of one's own needs and wants. Rescuing other people is an unhealthy lifestyle pattern. Don't make the mistake of feeling sorry for other people and then trying to meet their needs and wants. To do so is to deprive them of opportunity to increase their self-esteem and to grow by taking responsibility for their own needs and wants.

In Philip's case, his need to rescue damsels in distress was no accident. He was trying to boost his low self-esteem by saving women in dire need, and then expecting their adoration and undying gratitude. When he didn't get the appreciation and applause he expected, he lost interest in the woman. On those rare occasions when a woman actually expressed appreciation, it was never fulfilling enough to satisfy Philip.

No one can fulfill our wants and needs, but ourselves.

What Do You Want?

All of this is really good news. If you've been feeling unfulfilled and weren't sure how to remedy the situation, we'll take some time to clarify what you want. If you already know what you want, but have felt unsure about whether or not it was okay to fulfill that want, let's work on removing that block in your thinking.

There's an old adage: Be careful what you ask for; because you just might get it. Every prize carries with it a certain price. So it's important to ask yourself questions like: What do I really want? What am I willing to do to obtain it? Will it be worth having? Is it good for me? Am I willing to take the risk to achieve it? Do I understand that every prize carries a price?

Self-confidence is also an important factor. People with low self-confidence will hesitate to set "want goals" for themselves. They don't believe they're smart enough, educated enough, rich enough, talented enough—whatever enough—to achieve their goals. These are the people who will feel very unfulfilled, but lock themselves into a cycle, as well. They feel something is missing in their lives. However, they fail to crystallize in their own minds what that something is; they may blame a spouse for their lack of fulfillment, or, they may try to manipulate other people into fulfilling their wants for them.

The underlying cycle is that until people know what they want and take concrete steps toward fulfilling that want, their self-confidence will remain low.

Do you want more self-confidence? You'll get it by clarifying your want goals, and then acting in accordance with your wants. The responsibility raises your self-esteem.

Clarifying Your Want Goals

All accomplishments, whether minor or major, begin with an idea or a desire. Clarifying what you want and how to obtain it may be the most important questions you'll ever pose. Whatever your wants—recreation, education, income, health or love—they deserve your time and attention. Spend a few moments, right now, giving your wants some attention by going over the following steps toward goal achievement. These steps are the ingredients for fulfilling your wants.

1. Ask yourself, "What do I really want?"

This is an important starting point, because the only way to stay motivated to achieve a goal is a sincere desire to accomplishment it. Maybe you already know what you want. This exercise will simply give you the opportunity to begin working toward its accomplishment.

If you're unsure about what you want, your intuition

51

will give you answers. Go somewhere you can be alone, somewhere you won't be interrupted. A small, cozy room or a peaceful setting in nature—these are two ideal locations to meditate about your goals. Some people find it helpful to brainstorm first, by writing about their goals. Let yourself go. Just write your thoughts as you think of them, don't worry about spelling, grammar, or punctuation. As you write, your wants will start jumping off the page at you. Grab them!

Remember, as you are writing, you are responsible for fulfilling these want goals. Yet, you also must ask yourself, "How much control do I have over getting this want?" Most goals require the cooperation of other people. Your partner may also be affected by or need to participate in the fulfillment of your goal. Other people are factors we cannot control. We can only control our own thoughts and actions.

2. Write down your specific wants.

Studies conducted by business schools and insurance companies resoundingly point to the importance of writing goals. The power of writing a goal is astonishing. Yet many people procrastinate this step, because they fear committing themselves to a goal, and they also fear falling short or failing to reach a goal. The cure to this procrastination: force yourself to write these goals. There's no better time than the present.

Make your goals measurable and specific. Instead of writing "I want more money," write exactly how much money you plan to earn, as well as the exact amount of your annual income and savings goal. Your goal must also be obtainable. If someone wrote down a goal to increase their income by one thousand percent within one month, the subconscious mind would reject the goal as not achievable, and your income would stay the same.

3. Visualize your goal as becoming a reality.

This step helps in two ways: It solidifies your commitment to the goal, and, it helps fuel the excitement and motivation necessary to achieve the goal. Spend a few moments alone, letting yourself feel, see, and experience the achievement of your goal. Close your eyes and experience the goal as if it were true this very moment.

4. Pay attention to any negative thoughts or fears that appear.

This is valuable information, it provides clues to why your wants haven't been fulfilled. Fear is a powerful emotion that blocks goal achievement. Another block is a lack of self-confidence. This belief that you can't do it, becomes a self-fulfilling prophecy. Blocks and fears can be turned into valuable tools with the use of the fifth step in goal achievement.

5. Replace negative thoughts and fears with self-loving affirmations and memories of your past successes.

You hit the winning run for Little League. You groomed your 4-H animal into a blue ribbon champion. You gave the speech and received thunderous applause. Recalling your past achievements is a healthy way to boost confidence in your abilities to achieve goals.

Another confidence-boosting method is positive self-talk, the equivalent of a pep talk with yourself. Affirmations are one of the best ways to increase the belief that a goal can be achieved. Listen to recorded cassette tapes of affirmations, or customize your own version with personalized affirmations. If you prefer, write down your affirmations. Listen to, or read, your affirmations at least once a day. Within two weeks, you'll find that your self-confidence has increased. By the end of one month, your self-belief in your abilities will be much stronger. And with self-confidence, any goal can be accomplished.

Below are examples of affirmations that boost self-confidence.

- I have enough time, energy, and intelligence to accomplish all my desires.
- I am safe and secure.
- I am competent and creative.
- I am a winner.
- When I win, others win as well.
- It's okay for me to be good to myself.

Along the same lines, it's important to surround yourself with positive people. Don't discuss your goals with negative people. Negative people display toxic envy. They can't stand it when others achieve happiness or success: it threatens their negative belief system, and makes them feel like failures. Negative people would rather thwart your goals than risk making goals of their own. Attacking your goals brings you down and them up. They believe they are better than you, and, thus more deserving.

6. Review your goals on a regular basis.

To keep your goals as alive in six months as they are today, read them every day. My clients find it useful to post their written goals in a place they visit daily—on the bathroom mirror, in their office, or on a kitchen cabinet. Ideally, look at your resolutions more than once a day.

7. Break down your goals.

A major reason many goals aren't even attempted is because they seem overwhelming. To combat this intimidation, divide your goals into bite-sized chunks. For example, Melissa wanted to complete her M.B.A. degree. She divided her goal into smaller units, beginning with: "Call the university and make an appointment to see the admissions counselor." Melissa followed this step with: "Make an appointment for school registration," followed by, "Register for classes."

Remember; every big success is comprised of many small, achievable steps.

8. Work toward the accomplishment of your goal every day.

No matter what, complete one step every day toward making your resolution a reality. What you do is not as important as keeping your momentum alive. Do something every day that leads you toward your dream: read a book, make a telephone call, write a letter. As long as you keep your dream alive, and as long as you work toward its accomplishment, your want will become a reality!

The Eight Steps of Goal Achievement (and Self-Fulfillment)

1. Ask yourself, "What do I really want?"
   a) Will it be worth having?
   b) Is it good for me?
   c) What am I willing to do to obtain it?
   d) What must I risk to achieve it?
   e) Do I understand that every prize has a price?

2. Write down your specific wants.
   a) Keep them measurable and achievable.

3. Visualize your goal as already becoming a reality.

4. Pay attention to any negative thoughts or fears that appear.
   a) Don't allow the envy of others to distract you.
   b) Associate with people who are supportive of your goals. Avoid those who are not.

5. Replace negative thoughts and fears with self-loving affirmations and memories of past successes.

6. Review your goals on a regular basis.

7. Break down your goals.

8. Complete at least one step—big or small—toward the accomplishment of your goal every day.

TWENTY-FIVE SIGNS OF AN UNHEALTHY RELATIONSHIP

A relationship is either healthy or unhealthy, functional or dysfunctional. Often, people in dysfunctional relationships aren't aware that their partnership interactions are dysfunctional. They are only aware of the dissatisfaction they feel. When one or both partners engage in the following behaviors, it's a signal that the relationship may be dysfunctional.

1. *Attempts to control another person's behavior* — Controlling behavior can be obvious, such as with threats of violence or yelling. It can also be subtle: manipulating with guilt, coercion, or crying; or withholding sex, money or affection from a partner, as a way of extracting compliance.

2. *Putting the partner's needs and wants first, at the expense of self-fulfillment* — In an unhealthy relationship, there is this underlying belief: "If I

57

sacrifice my own happiness for you, I expect you always to love me in return."

3. *A strong desire to be needed by one's partner, and equating need with love* — Needy people feel unloved, threatened, and jealous if their partner engages in separate activities. Of course, it would be normal to feel jealous if one's partner, for example, went alone to a singles bar. But needy people feel threatened when their partner engages in ordinary activities, such as golfing, reading, or shopping.

4. *Not confronting the unsuitable behavior of a partner* — In an unhealthy relationship, there is a fear of being honest and authentic with one another. For example, a woman who loathes her husband's excessive gambling doesn't confront him because she fears her husband's screaming and yelling. A man, upset about his wife's misuse of credit cards, doesn't confront her out of fear that she'll withhold sex.

5. *A tendency to deny or rationalize one's feelings* — People perpetuate a dysfunctional relationship by pretending—to themselves and their partners—that everything is fine. Although they feel hurt, betrayed, and angry inside, they fear admitting these emotions because they then have to do something to correct the situation. They feel it is easier to pretend. Of course, in the long run, such pretending makes life much more difficult and much less satisfying. Pretenders don't have real relationships, they have pseudo-rela-

tionships. A partner can only be in love with you if you show your partner who you really are.

6. *A feeling of not being good enough, or feeling unworthy*— People with high self-esteem do not tolerate a dysfunctional relationship for long. They either get out, take steps to resolve the problems, or allow their self-esteem to drop in order to stay in the dysfunctional relationship.

7. *Self-esteem is dependent on the approval of others* — "If you compliment me, then I like myself; if you criticize me, I must be a bad person"—these are the underlying beliefs of partners in a dysfunctional relationship. When you allow external factors (other people's opinions, your school grades, your weight, etc.) to determine your self-esteem, you can't have high self-esteem. Healthy self-esteem is only possible when you have a great working partnership with yourself.

8. *An intense fear of criticism or anger, and avoidance—at all costs—of confrontations or quarrels* — For example: one partner walks around on eggshells to avoid accidentally incurring the other partner's wrath. Or, one partner avoids voicing any opinion that clashes with that of the other partner.

9. *A fear of letting the partner know one's true feelings or other parts of oneself*— This comes from the belief: "To know me is to reject me"—a belief leading a partner to shield their true opinions and desires from the other partner. Such people

edit and censor their words rather than freely communicating their thoughts and feelings.

10. *An intense fear of being hurt by one's partner* — The fear of emotional pain is perfectly normal, in fact most of us actively seek ways to avoid pain. The difference between healthy and unhealthy avoidance of pain is whether or not you let the fear of pain stop you from correcting an unacceptable situation. In a dysfunctional relationship, the fear of being hurt is so intense and overwhelming that the fear actually dictates a person's actions. That person is controlled and paralyzed by his or her own fear. The sad irony is that their worst fears of being emotionally hurt often come true because dysfunctional relationships inflict pain for both partners.

11. *Difficulty in identifying one's own feelings* — They know they feel bad, but they are not sure whether they are sad or angry. Outer-focused people are unaware of their true emotions. They are exquisitely aware of others' feelings—a survival mechanism they have developed—yet, their own self-awareness is blocked.

12. *Feeling responsible for the partner's feelings or behavior* — This is another irony intrinsic in dysfunctional relationships: a partner feels weak or powerless over his or her own life—but at the same time, feels completely responsible for ensuring the happiness of everyone around him or her. If a wife sees that her husband is upset, she berates herself for somehow failing.

13. *Agreeing with your partner, even when you really disagree, for the sake of maintaining peace* — Agreeing, just to keep the peace, becomes chronic and habitual. The lack of honesty and authenticity is poisonous to the relationship. Yes-Men and Yes-Women may be easy to get along with, but underneath they feel misunderstood, used, and afraid. Their over-compliance erodes their self-respect and self-love.

14. *Rather than negotiating solutions to problems, manipulating, forcing, or coercing in order to get one's way* — Underneath this behavior is fear and mistrust. A healthy partner assumes, "I can honestly and directly tell my partner what I think, what I want, and what I need. She may not agree with me, but at least we'll both know where the other stands. That's the only way to arrive at a creative solution." The dysfunctional partner, in contrast, fears, "If I reveal what I really want, my partner will use it against me. I'll have to trick my partner into giving me what I want."

15. *Frequent criticism of a partner* — An overly-critical partner may have one of the following agendas:

- "I need my partner to be perfect, because she is a reflection of my self-worth. I'll tell her how to improve herself, so that I will look better to other people."
- "My partner's self-confidence is getting too high. I'm afraid he'll leave me if he realizes that he's

better than me. I'll knock his ego down a few notches, so he'll stay humble and stay with me."

- "I'm angry at my partner for hurting my feelings. I'll get revenge and hurt her feelings by saying something mean about her."

16. *Feeling defensive of one's self or behavior* — Defensive people think that other people are criticizing or rejecting them, when no evidence exists to support these conclusions. They expect to be criticized, so they read disapproval into neutral comments.

17. *Withdrawing, avoiding and distancing from one another* — In a dysfunctional relationship, both partners pull away from one another as a protective measure. They are more like strangers, or roommates, than like relationship partners.

18. *Displaying obvious contempt for one another* — A husband makes verbal jabs at his wife when they're at cocktail parties. She slings stinging words at him when others are around. This couple—straight out of *Who's Afraid of Virginia Woolf?*—is attempting to communicate with one another through harsh words. The underlying message is: "You've hurt me. I'm angry with you. I don't respect you." But that hurt is covered up with hate and anger.

Dysfunctional partners compete negatively with one another and have a "need to win." You've probably met a couple like this before. The man is always trying to one-up his wife, and she's constantly correcting him. Both partners are always trying to outdo one another, in the unhealthy belief that: "If I'm better than you, I'll feel better about myself in comparison. I'll squash you to elevate myself."

19. *Rationalizing or making excuses for a partner's dysfunctional behavior* — A partner blames themselves or outside circumstances for their partner's unacceptable behavior. Rather than confront Maggie's excessive drinking, her husband, Fred, rationalizes, "She's under a lot of stress lately. As soon as her schedule eases, she won't drink as much." In a similar case, Sally excused her husband's abusive screaming and cursing by thinking, "I deserve it. He wouldn't be so angry if I'd just act better."

20. *Using guilt-trips to control a partner* — Karen didn't want her fiancé, Larry, to go away for his weekend of hunting and fishing. She didn't want to be left alone with nothing to do for two days. Karen had two healthy options for dealing with her discomfort: She could have confronted herself, discovering why she feared being alone. Then, Karen might have made plans to fill her free time with activities personally meaningful to her, or, Karen could have shared her feelings directly with Larry, making it clear that she was not asking him to cancel his hunting trip. Her purpose for sharing would be to express her sentiments, and maybe to hear some reassuring words from Larry.

Unfortunately, Karen reacted in a dysfunctional manner to her fears of being alone; she laid a guilt trip on Larry trying to manipulate him into canceling his trip. She said, "A good man would-n't leave his fiancé alone," "Maybe I'll get dressed up and go to a nightclub while you're gone," and "Don't worry about me [heavy sigh]. I'll be just fine all alone." Larry went on his trip anyway, but felt resentful and confused by Karen's behavior.

21. *Screaming or yelling loudly, to purposely intimi-date and control the partner* — When one or both partners act like a bully, there's little room for emotional intimacy. Yelling *may* result in one partner getting his or her way, but respect for one another—and one's own self for being a bully or being bullied—is eroded. Often, bullied partners feel they must walk around on eggshells to avoid their partner's wrath. If neither partner feels safe to be authentic, the relationship is dys-functional.

22. *Giving up friends or interests outside of the rela-tionship* — partners in a dysfunctional relation-ship become isolated from the outside world for many different reasons:

- The fear of criticism: Patricia and Bill stayed away from others because they didn't want their marijuana smoking habit discovered or criticized.
- The fear of comparisons. Ever since Henry's job demotion last year, he and Candice stopped socializing with other couples. They felt badly about their financial problems, and

avoided the company of anyone who was prospering.

- The fear of infidelity. When Sheri and Mark first dated, she had an active social life. She was a member of the Junior League, an avid tennis player and pursued many other activities with her friends. When they became engaged, Mark asked Sheri to spend less time with her friends—100 percent less. He feared losing her to another man. Sheri agreed to Mark's request for fear of losing Mark if she didn't comply.

23. *Resenting the other person for not making you happy* — These include the following beliefs:

- "If it wasn't for you, I could ____ (have more fun, pursue my hobbies and interests, be more successful in my career, lose weight, and so on)."
- "If my partner would only make more money, we would be a lot happier."
- "If my partner really loved me, she would know what I want. She would instinctively know how to make me happy, without my having to tell her."
- "I would love to pursue a hobby, or further my education, but my partner won't let me."
- "If only I weren't married, I could have the freedom and great sex life that I'm missing right now."
- "A real man would give me expensive gifts, take me to great restaurants, and on wonderful vacations."

24. *Not telling a trusted confidant about trouble in the relationship* — (This is also pretending that everything is perfect to the outside world.) Dianna was afraid to tell anyone about her explosive fights with Jim. "They have worries of their own," explained Dianna. But the fights became more intense, at times physical. Still, Dianna didn't tell anyone. In therapy, Dianna finally realized she feared being viewed as less than perfect by others. As her self-esteem plummeted from the episodes of abuse, Dianna's need to be viewed favorably seemed even more essential to her. At the therapist's urging, Dianna went to a domestic violence shelter and worked on her self-esteem.

25. *Telling only a trusted confidant, rather than confronting your partner, about the trouble in the relationship* — In direct contrast to Dianna's situation is Brenda's: Brenda is having doubts about her relationship with her fiancé, Robert. She wonders whether the marriage will last, and whether it will be mutually fulfilling. But rather than share her doubts and confusions with Robert, Brenda pours her heart out to everyone else: her girlfriends, her mother, her therapist, even her hairdresser. But the one person who could really provide input or solutions—namely Robert—does not know that Brenda is feeling ambivalent toward their fast-approaching wedding. (I do not advocate confronting your partner if that person is unstable—that is, exhibits behavior that is influenced by alcohol, drugs, or hysteria, or if physical violence exists in the rela-

tionship. Your safety is more important. Your partner needs professional care and you must seek professional help from either a shelter, clinic, or private practitioner.)

Twenty-five Signs of an Unhealthy Relationship

1. Attempts to control a partner's behavior
2. Putting a partner's needs and wants ahead of one's own self-fulfillment
3. A strong desire to be needed by one's partner, and equating need with love
4. Not confronting the unsuitable behavior in one's partner
5. A tendency to deny or rationalize one's feelings
6. A feeling of not being good enough, feeling unworthy
7. Self-esteem is dependent on a partner's approval
8. An intense fear of criticism or anger, and avoidance—at all costs—of confrontations or quarrels
9. A fear of letting the partner know one's true feelings or other aspects of oneself
10. An intense fear of being hurt by one's partner
11. Difficulty in identifying one's own feelings
12. Feeling responsible for a partner's feelings or behavior
13. Agreeing with your partner when you really disagree for the sake of peacekeeping.
14. Rather than negotiating solutions to problems, manipulating, forcing, or coercing in order to get one's own way
15. Frequent criticism of a partner
16. Feeling defensive of one's self or behavior
17. Withdrawing, avoiding, and distancing from one another
18. Displaying obvious contempt for one another
19. Rationalizing or making excuses for a partner's dysfunctional behavior
20. Using guilt trips to control a partner.
21. Screaming or yelling to purposely intimidate and control a partner
22. Giving up friends or interests outside of the relationship.
23. Resenting the other person for not making you happy.
24. Not telling a trusted confidant about trouble in your relationship (pretending everything is perfect)
25. Not confronting a partner (If a history of violence exists, confrontation could be dangerous. Seek professional help from a shelter, clinic, or private practitioner.)

TWENTY-FIVE SIGNS OF A HEALTHY RELATIONSHIP

An **unhealthy** relationship tears the partners down, a healthy relationship stimulates both partners' individual growth. A functional relationship acts like a human greenhouse, encouraging and nurturing a person to flourish and grow. A functional relationship is not a fairy-tale type "they lived happily ever after" scenario; it is subject to the same stresses and challenges inherent in any human partnership. The important distinction between a functional and a dysfunctional relationship is this: the former encourages personal growth (constructive), while the latter discourages personal growth (destructive). Below are the signs of a functional relationship:

1.   *Encouraging one another to develop new skills and interests* — Healthy relationship partners delight in seeing each other's happiness and excitement. They feel stimulated and intrigued by their partner's growing knowledge and confi-

dence. They find each new experiences fascinating, and they encourage each other's continued growth. In a healthy relationship, the two partners promote the development of each other's potential.

2. *Emotionally supporting one another's goals* — Forty-seven-year-old Lorraine has decided to complete her bachelor's degree, now that her three children are grown and on their own. It was a difficult decision for Lorraine, given her age and her competing desire to travel. Her husband, Sean, fully supports Lorraine's decision to return to school. He will be there to encourage her during the inevitable moments of doubt, frustration, and stress—as well as during her moments of excitement and happiness. (Sean will also be there during summer breaks, as they travel to Europe together).

3. *Not feeling threatened by a partner's outside interests* — When Chris told his wife, Ada, that he wanted to buy a Harley-Davidson motorcycle, she was surprised at first and a little confused. Ada had no interest in motorcycle riding—the thought of riding on the back of a bike scared her enormously. The couple discussed the situation, and agreed that: Chris would take a motorcycle safety course; Ada would not be pressured to ride the motorcycle or participate in the Harley-Davidson group activities; Chris could enjoy his motorcycle without Ada; and Ada would take responsibility for filling up her time apart from Chris. By discussing and negotiating

their separate interests, neither Ada nor Chris were resentful or reluctant to pursue their own pleasures.

4. *Trusting one another* — Trust is having the confidence in your judgment to trust yourself to trust your partner. I distinguish between earned trust versus blind trust. Children blindly trust their parents to provide for them. As adults, we learn to trust through self-awareness. Our mates earn trust by demonstrating they are trustworthy. Their actions—not just their words—are consistent with behavior we know to be healthy. Trust is central for a relationship's health. In a functional relationship, both partners trust themselves to trust each other. They know their partner will

    *   remain loyal and monogamous
    *   not be abusive, emotionally or physically
    *   keep their promises, and be reliable
    *   pull their own weight in meeting the couple's goals and obligations
    *   be honest and not lie or mislead
    *   not intentionally inflict pain on the other partner
    *   openly and directly share their feelings, thoughts, and opinions with the other partner

    When you trust your partner, you will be safe. You know you won't be hurt, betrayed, or ridiculed. In this setting of trust, you can let down your guard and really be yourself with your partner, allowing a feeling of safety to flow through their relationship. You don't need to censor or edit your conversations, or alter your behavior (as long as your words and behavior are kind and courteous). You can open your heart to the other person. This deep trust and mutual vulnerability forms the core of lasting love. It is the essence of intimacy: "I can deeply trust myself to feel safe with you."

5. *Responding to problems with the goal of negotiating solutions* — Whenever two people spend time together, there are bound to be occasional differences of opinion. The *way* these differences are resolved can mean the difference between a functional and a dysfunctional relationship. Carole, for example, felt her husband, Darren, was spending too much time at his law practice, and not enough time with her and their two young children. The children asked, "Where's Daddy?" so frequently, that Carole decided to negotiate a solution with Darren. The couple discussed ways that Darren could fulfill both his career and his family responsibilities. They hit upon a creative, workable solution: Carole would pitch in to help Darren meet his deadlines. This would give the couple time together, as well as free up Darren's weekends so that the family could enjoy pleasurable leisure time.

6. *Taking responsibility for one's role in any relationship problems* — When one partner says, "I would like to talk about something," the other partner in a healthy relationship is open and available. If necessary they will schedule an

appointment and then adhere to the appointment. In a dysfunctional relationship, "We need to talk" is usually met with defensiveness, such as "I didn't do anything wrong!" or with distancing, as in "Oh, honey you know how much I hate to talk about our problems."

7. *Fulfilling one's own needs and wants* — At age forty-five, Chuck had a deep yearning to perform volunteer work with the disadvantaged and homeless people his community. He found deep satisfaction in working at the soup kitchen and performing fund-raising activities. His wife, Sarah, respected Chuck's volunteer work and emotionally supported him, although choosing not to personally participate.

   Another couple, Cindy and Frank, had a similar experience. Cindy had always dreamed of being a professional potter, creating mugs and vases in her backyard and selling them in an in-home pottery boutique. But through the years, Cindy had ignored her dream and had, instead, built a successful career as a bank manager. On her thirty-fifth birthday, Cindy underwent a personal crisis in which she questioned her career and her life's work. She made a decision, and created a plan to fulfill her dreams: Cindy would work on her pottery at night, with the goal of easing out of her banking job and supporting herself gradually with her pottery work. Cindy took responsibility for meeting her own wants and dreams in a realistic and achievable manner. Frank used the time to work on some of his unfinished projects.

8. *Not blaming the partner for your own unhappiness* — "Something is missing from my life"—it's a thought most of us have from time to time. It's a normal thought that can propel us either toward growth and fulfillment, or toward destructive blaming patterns. Functional people take action to resolve their feelings of dissatisfaction. Dysfunctional people, in contrast, blame their partner for their unhappiness. Functional people says to themselves, "What am I doing, or not doing, that is contributing to my dissatisfaction?" Dysfunctional people say, "I'd be more satisfied if only my partner would change."

9. *Openly sharing feelings with one another in a responsible, non-abusive manner* — Tricia and Steve rarely disagreed with one another during their six-year marriage, until the birth of their son, Andrew, two years ago. Now, Tricia and Steve are having difficulty seeing eye to eye on child-rearing practices. "Steve wants to raise Andrew with this controlling, disciplinarian method," Tricia complained to her counselor. "I think we should raise Andrew in a setting of loving acceptance, where we're encouraging him instead of yelling at him."

In a dysfunctional relationship, the couple would try to resolve their differences of opinion with screams, threats and name-calling. The couple would use "tactics" such as yelling, guilt trips, or manipulation to get their way. These tactics don't resolve situations in a satisfactory manner.

Contrast those tactics with the healthy measures

Tricia and Steve used. They discussed the basis of their child-rearing philosophies. Steve said he was raised by strict parents "adding I turned out fine, didn't I?" Tricia talked about the hands-off policy her own parents had used during her childhood. In discussing how to raise Andrew, both Steve and Tricia discovered something important: neither of them really liked the extreme parenting style they'd been raised with. They mutually decided to enroll in a parenting class held at a nearby adult education class.

10. *Having regard for one another's feelings* — In the heat of an argument, it's important to attack the issue and not the person. Even when emotions run high avoid hurling insults. Those words can fracture the delicate balance of trust within a relationship, and can cause irrevocable damage.

    Even in the cool of normal, everyday interactions within a relationship, healthy partners know the importance of treating one another with respect and kindness. It's sad, but we sometimes afford more courtesy to strangers than to our own mate! Long-term, fulfilling relationships are constructed upon a solid foundation of mutual respect and the golden rule. Treating our partners with respect doesn't occur by accident; it's a choice and a decision.

11. *Respecting and encouraging the partner's individuality* — When Natalie told her husband, Richard, that she wanted to attend church regularly, he was entirely supportive. Natalie explained that she'd been craving spiritual

enrichment and stimulation, and knew that attending church would fulfill this desire. Richard discussed how he respected and supported Natalie, and appreciated her not pushing him to go with her. He explained how he'd felt forced to attend church as a child. As an adult, he preferred to pray outside a church setting. Richard explained that if he reconciled his feelings he would go to church with Natalie. In the meantime, both partners supported the other's position. Richard would support Natalie's desire to attend church, and Natalie would honor Richard's decision to stay home.

It's unrealistic to expect our love partner to be our identical twin. He or she is bound to have priorities that differ from our own. The way those differences are handled is one distinction between a healthy and an unhealthy relationship. In a unhealthy relationship, differences are viewed as threats or a sign that "this isn't my dream lover after all." In healthy relationships, differences are discussed, negotiated, and supported.

12. *Maintaining one's boundaries* — Both partners in a healthy relationship know that the partnership is only as healthy as the individual partners. In chapter 10, I further explain the nature and necessity of boundaries. Basically, a person with healthy boundaries knows the following:

   • "I am an individual separate from you."
   • "I have the right to my own, separate life."
   • "I have the right to maintain secrets, as long

as I'm not being dishonest or harming you in any way."

- "I am responsible for meeting my needs."
- "I am responsible for expressing my wants and negotiating for their attainment."

13. *Maintaining one's integrity and self-respect* — Taking care of yourself is an investment that pays dividends in your love relationship. Self-respect is earned by acting in accordance with your beliefs and values. If you act against your deepest beliefs, you will lose respect for yourself. If you act as you believe (something only you can decide for yourself), you heighten and maintain self-respect.

    Have you ever been in a relationship with a person who has lower self-esteem than you do? Most of us have; and as you've probably already discovered, this type of relationship is doomed from the outset. A healthy relationship requires two partners with healthy levels of self-esteem. Each partner has an obligation to continue doing whatever is necessary to maintain their individual integrity.

14. *Being willing to invest time and energy toward helping the relationship* — At the first sign of problems or conflict, a dysfunctional person will run for the hills. A healthy relationship takes effort and some emotional elbow grease, it is something that requires a commitment from both partners. This is not to say a healthy relationship is one, long prison sentence of continuing conflict. Actually, a long-term healthy relationship is

much less stressful than a series of short-term, dysfunctional relationships. The former is growth-producing; the latter shreds people's lives apart.

Individuals must make their own decisions about this issue. What is your choice when dealing with problems or conflicts within the relationship? If your partner is non-abusive, and is healthy and compatible with you, will you stick it out through the hard times? Is a fulfilling relationship enough of a prize for you to pay the price of some effort and occasional discomfort, in order to nurture and maintain the partnership?

Again, I want to stress that I'm not talking about playing the role of a Martyr or a Victim. We've already seen the futility and unhealthiness of playing those roles. I'm talking about facing problems head-on, negotiating solutions and then doing the necessary follow-up work.

15. *Maintaining honesty and credibility* — Cassandra and Mark, who have been dating for two years, are discussing the possibility of moving in together. Cassandra is having some doubts because she believes living together outside of marriage is both immoral and unwise. "My parents are dead set against what they call living in sin," Cassandra told her best friend. "But Mark says he won't be ready to get married until we've first tested how compatible we are together. I'm afraid if I don't go along with him he'll break up with me."

This couple is already in trouble. Cassandra and Mark are neither ready to either live together, nor ready for marriage. The fact that Cassandra isn't honest with Mark about her fundamental beliefs is a hallmark of a dysfunctional relationship. In a healthy relationship, Cassandra and Mark would openly discuss their feelings and beliefs. They would negotiate a solution such as:

- They could attend premarital counseling, to explore whether or not their wants, values, and goals, were indeed compatible.
- They could set a future wedding date, and wait to live together until after the marriage ceremony.
- They could move in together, with an agreement that they will live separately if they aren't married within a set period of time.
- They could decide they aren't compatible, and break up.

16. *Being giving, in healthy ways* — What do men and women long for, more than anything else? Not expensive presents or trips (although those are certainly appreciated). What men and women really want is a thoughtful, loving partner who is willing to negotiate an equitable relationship.

Examples of giving in a healthy manner:

- Each respects the other's values and style.
- Each tries to understand their partner's point of view and will support the other's right to hold differing opinions.
- Each strives for equality in the relationship;

79

neither assumes a superior role such as that of a parent and a child.
- Each remembers the other's special and unique pleasures.
- Neither patronizes nor placates the other with insincere compliments.

17. *Being monogamous and loyal* — A relationship cannot survive when the partners are putting their energy into other sexual or romantic partners. Although I've worked with many couples who have salvaged their marriage after one partner admitted to an affair, the relationship is always threatened by such an event. Breaking a commitment to exclusivity hurts relationships in so many ways:

- The person committing the act of infidelity loses self-respect.
- Trust is broken, thus destroying intimacy.
- The deceitful partner takes away time and energy from the primary relationship.
- The partner who was deceived has been betrayed. This betrayal is interpreted as a symbol that, "You do not respect me. You do not value me. You do not value a commitment."

Infidelity is a symptom of underlying, unresolved issues within the individual and within the relationship. In a healthy relationship, those issues are never left unresolved. The benefits of fidelity are valued within a healthy relationship. Both partners know they stand to gain much more, by

80

remaining monogamous, than they could ever gain by sleeping around.

Monogamy helps partners build trust and friendship. It fosters a sense of permanency and stability—qualities often lacking in our unstable world. At a time when people can't count on job security, or social security, the feeling of relationship security is even more valuable.

18. *Being willing to confront dysfunctional or unacceptable behavior* — Nobody enjoys conflict, except the unhealthy person who views fighting as an exciting and dramatic sport. It's equally unhealthy, however, to be so conflict-phobic that all confrontations are shunned and avoided.

A healthy relationship is built on a mutual agreement to bring problems to the table for discussion and negotiation. Much like a business meeting where partners look for ways to increase profits, healthy love partners discuss ways to increase fulfillment.

Last year, forty-four-year-old Stan was transferred to another division of his company. He received a raise, but along with the extra money, Stan was expected to work fifty and sixty hour weeks. His wife, Mildred, was grateful for Stan's increased pay, but was upset that Stan had gotten unreasonably sloppy around the house. He stopped cleaning up after himself in the kitchen, and began leaving his dirty clothes on the bathroom floor.

How would Mildred handle this situation in an unhealthy and in a healthy relationship?

Unhealthy responses

- Mildred would call Stan names. ("You're such a slob!")
- Mildred would play the Martyr/Victim role and pick up after Stan, while stuffing her resentment of his behavior.
- Mildred would try to rationalize the situation. ("He's making more money and working hard; I shouldn't expect him to help me around the house.")
- Mildred would act passive-aggressively. For example, she would wash Stan's dirty clothes, found on the bathroom floor, in bleach and hot water and "accidentally" ruin them.
- Mildred would try to punish or teach Stan a lesson by allowing the dirty clothes and dishes to accumulate. This would be the equivalent of Mildred taking a parenting role with Stan, however. It is not an honest, healthy expression of her feelings. What's more, Mildred would suffer from this treatment, since the kitchen and bathroom are "her" areas, as well as Stan's.
- Mildred would punish Stan by withdrawing expressions of affection and sex.

Healthy responses

- Mildred would confront the unacceptable behavior in an adult, non-abusive way. ("Stan, I feel frustrated because your dirty clothes are on the bathroom floor. I wonder why you're suddenly doing this. I also want to talk about resolving it, because I don't want to clean up after you and I don't want to look at the mess.")

- Stan and Mildred would discuss solutions, such as using some of the extra money Stan is earning to hire a cleaning crew, or, more likely Stan taking responsibility for his mess and cleaning up after himself.

19. *Being intimate with the partner and the relationship* — A healthy partnership is a safe haven where both partners are free to be themselves without censor or worry. They are thoughtful and kind toward one another, but they don't pretend to be someone other than who they are. This is called intimacy, the ability to trust your relationship.

Most of us have jobs that keep us a little on guard all day long. It's not wise, for example, to be completely authentic with your boss when you think he's making an idiotic company decision. It's probably not a good idea to level with your best customer who happens to be a jerk— unless you own the company or have a new job lined up. It's also best not to confront the officer who is writing your speeding ticket.

When we are together with our partner, however, the healthy relationship nurtures our authentic self. We let go and trust. We experience the feeling of being in a safe environment.

20. *Pulling one's fair share and negotiating responsibilities* — In a functional relationship, neither partner takes advantage of the other person's

time or money. Both partners assume responsibility for fulfilling the couple's mutual needs and wants, such as a clean house, sufficient income, keeping cars in proper working order and eating nutritious meals.

This isn't to say that every couple will achieve an ideal fifty-fifty arrangement—that may not be realistic or even desirable. Both partners should concentrate on performing the tasks they are best suited for or those they are most interested in doing.

Sometimes, these tasks defy traditional notions about gender: Belinda and Tom have what some would call a nontraditional marriage. Belinda is the bread winner, and she loves it! Her job as the co-host of a morning radio show gives her enjoyment, stimulation and plenty of money. Tom enjoys staying home with their infant son, and taking care of the household duties. Belinda pitches in when she gets home in the early afternoon. Both partners are content that their individual, and mutual, needs and wants are being met.

In two-career families, duties should be performed on an as-needed basis. The days of women doing all the housework ended with demise of the 1950s-style sitcoms and the stereotypical male/female roles. If a man wants a full-time housekeeper, he is free to hire one. His wife, however, is likely among the majority of American women who work outside the home. And that means he needs to do more around the house than merely lifting his feet off the floor as she vacuums next to the sofa.

Both partners are responsible for confronting and negotiating their own needs and wants. If a woman feels harried and overworked, she is 100 percent responsible for teaching her husband what she wants.

21. *Showing thoughtfulness and common courtesy* — I've observed that people are often kinder to strangers than they are to their own spouses. They stop using terms of politeness such as please and thank you. We don't have to be stuffed-shirt or formal around our mates, but they are still human beings. And every human being deserves thoughtfulness.

    "But my husband's not polite to me!" Sheryl argued when I talked with her about this issue. "If he was nice to me, I would certainly treat him better." This stand-off, or impasse, is impossible to break unless one person agrees to go first. It's possible to "melt the ice" of years and years of mutual impoliteness, if one partner begins exercising consistent courtesy.

    Is courtesy important to you? Your definitions of how you want to be treated are part of your boundaries. It's necessary to confront your partner when his or her behavior is not acceptable to you. This is information to share and negotiate with your partner. No matter how many years you've been together, you can change the dynamics of your relationship to meet your own wants.

    Examples of thoughtful behavior between two love partners:

- telephoning to say you are going to be late
- asking your partner before making plans for the two of you
- talking with your partner about any plan or activity (having company over, making a major purchase; changing careers, and so on) that will impact both of you
- asking, "Are you watching this program?" before switching television channels
- keeping a low volume on radio or television programs when your partner is in need of quiet
- saying please and thank you. (This will make you feel good, too!)
- helping or assisting without complaining or attempting to control

22. *Using active-listening skills* — This includes eye contact and letting your partner finish a thought before you reply. It's a common situation: a man is reading a newspaper while his wife is talking. She complains, "You're not listening to me!" The man responds, "Yes I am," and then recites every word she has said, verbatim.

Active listening is more than hearing the spoken words. It is actively letting the other person know you are interested in what they have to say. Active-listening skills include

- looking your partner in eye
- saying appropriate "uh-hms" or other indications you are listening
- leaning slightly toward your partner to signal your interest

- asking questions to get more information, and to show interest
- Summarizing what you heard your partner say (This is one of the greatest gifts you can give your partner. It feels great to be heard and understood.)
- Waiting until your partner is finished talking before replying (Interruptions communicate lack of empathy for your partner's opinions).

23. *Taking action to overcome problems* — Couples newly in love sometimes blissfully wonder, "Will we ever have problems?" The answer is a definite: yes. All couples have problems from time to time. Problems do not mean that you and your partner are incompatible, however.

    Incompatibility occurs only when a couple is unwilling to work on their problems. Action is always necessary to overcome problems that inevitably arise in a relationship. Action means any or all of the following:

    - telling your partner about your problem (confronting)
    - listening to your partner about his or her problem.
    - presenting your opinions and feelings about the problem (arguing).
    - deciding to work together to solve the problem, so that both partners are happy (negotiating).

24. *Committing to a long-term relationship* — Will you run the other way at the first sign of trouble?

Or, will you decide, "I am committed to making this relationship work," and take the time and expend the effort to negotiate a solution?

A healthy couple is committed to working together. Both partners realize that togetherness necessarily means having some differences in opinions. Healthy partners are ready to negotiate those differences, rather than turn away from them or compete to win.

25. *Working together toward mutual goals* — Healthy people have goals. These goals may involve raising a family, building a corporation, buying a certain type of house, or saving toward their retirement. Healthy couples intertwine personal goals. They work together for mutual fulfillment.

Bradley and Susan are saving 10 percent of each paycheck. Their mutual goal is a down payment on a two story house on the west side of town.

Candela and François want to have a baby, but they want to wait until the time is right. Candela wants to wait until she has graduated from college and established her career. François wants to wait until they have saved enough money to build a nursery in their house. They negotiate a time frame acceptable to both.

Camille and Henry are in their forties, and have set mutual goals for retirement. Both partners are contributing to their employers' 401-K plan; both have made a will; and both are saving toward their dream of traveling to Europe for their twenty-fifth wedding anniversary.

You are probably not surprised by the qualities of healthy relationships just described. Most people dream of having a high-quality relationship. They just don't know how to go about getting one. Your behavior determines whether you will have a healthy relationship, an unhealthy relationship, or no relationship. It is, and always has been, completely up to you.

If you choose to have a healthy relationship, you may feel some initial discomfort as you share your boundaries and wants with your partner. It can feel intimidating, at first, to expose your true self to another person. The fears run the gamut: "What if he rejects me?" to "What if she thinks I'm a wimp for wanting these things?"

If you want a fulfilling relationship, take Nike's advice and "Just do it!" No one said it would be easy. However, sharing your boundaries and wants with your partner does get easier over time. It becomes a positive habit.

Professional psychotherapy is often necessary. Most of the destructive habits brought into a relationship are rooted in childhood traumas. Through therapy, one gains awareness of the causes of the pain that produces the negative behavior in the relationship. This is the first step in learning how to let go, and to begin experiencing a fulfilling, positive relationship. It isn't easy. The process can be painful. But the rewards for the effort are definitely worth it. I firmly believe that, as difficult as it is to maintain a healthy relationship, an unhealthy relationship is even more stressful. Fighting, break-ups, and divorce are among the most painful and stressful of all events human beings can endure. By comparison, taking the steps to ensure that your present relationship is compatible and healthy is a welcome alternative!

25 Signs of a Healthy Relationship

1. Encouraging one another to develop new skills and interests
2. Emotionally supporting one another's goals
3. Not feeling threatened by a partner's outside interests
4. Trusting oneself to trust the other
5. Responding to problems by negotiating solutions
6. Taking responsibility for one's role in any relationship problem
7. Fulfilling one's own needs and wants
8. Not blaming a partner for one's own unhappiness
9. Establishing intimacy by openly sharing feelings with one another in a responsible, non-abusive manner
10. Having regard for the partner's feelings
11. Respecting and encouraging a partner's individuality
12. Maintaining the integrity of one's boundaries
13. Maintaining one's integrity and self-respect
14. Being willing to invest time and energy toward helping the relationship
15. Maintaining honesty and credibility
16. Being giving in healthy ways
17. Being monogamous and loyal
18. Being willing to confront dysfunctional or unacceptable behavior
19. Being intimate with a partner and the relationship
20. Pulling one's fair share, and negotiating responsibilities
21. Showing thoughtfulness and common courtesy (calling when late, etc.)
22. Using active listening skills
23. Taking action to overcome problems
24. Committing to a long-term relationship
25. Working together toward mutual goals

A Comparison Between Healthy and Unhealthy Relationship Characteristics

Healthy Relationship	*Unhealthy Relationship*
kindness	attacks
emotional support	rage
understanding	hysterics
vulnerability	control
respect	rescuing
trust	distrust
courtesy	dependency
cherishing	placating
honesty	dishonesty
monogamy	cheating or philander-
consideration	ing
continuity	withholding
equality	multiple break-ups
credibility	desire to win, or blame
	unreliability

CONTROL AND DEPENDENCY ISSUES

Power struggles, desires to control, and dependency issues are at the root of many conflicts and hurt feelings in relationships. Like two people struggling to gain control of the blanket on a bed, the partners are engaged in a war in which one will win and one will lose—and in the end, both will lose. Rather than cooperate for mutual satisfaction, controlling and submissive partners seem bent upon destroying one another, as well as the relationship.

This type of conflict stems from insecurity, defensiveness, and a need to be right. You cannot control an independent person. Therefore, a controlled person is, by definition, a dependent person.

Symbiotic Relationships

I cannot control you unless you *allow* me to. If you allow me to control you—for whatever reason—you

93

have a dependency on me. Codependency comes in when I have the desire to control you. It's not that you *want* to be controlled; it's just that you don't want to be abandoned or rejected. The underlying thought is: "I'll let you control me, if you promise not to leave me."

A healthy person will confront a controlling person. Take for example, a man who has a need to control, but is with a healthy woman who knows the score. If she confronts this man about his controlling behavior, and he doesn't believe he has a problem, can this relationship survive? No. These partners are incompatible; one is healthy, the other is not. This man has closed the door to possible negotiation because he denies that his behavior is inappropriate.

A compatible couple negotiates. A couple that refuses to negotiate is incompatible. Period.

Control is the act of imposing your will upon someone else. Abuse is the successful accomplishment of the act. This is very different from the healthy process of negotiating. Controlling behavior implies an urgent intent to manipulate the other person's behavior, by any means possible. Abuse almost always follows—emotional and often physical abuse. In negotiation, you share your thoughts, feelings, wants, and needs with your partner and discuss possible options leading to solutions.

If I submit to your demands for control, either by placating you or rescuing you, I'm really not a healthy person. It's impossible to have a good relationship if one or both people are unhealthy. A healthy relationship is only possible when both partners respect themselves and their partners.

When it comes to controlling behavior, there are three combinations possible in a relationship:

Control	Negotiation
"I want you to change to suit me."	"I want you to respect and understand me."
"I will use whatever means necessary to get you to conform to my wishes."	"I want us to work together to find suitable solutions."
"If I don't get my way, I will punish you."	"I realize that our mutual decisions may involve some negotiating."
"After I tell you my opinion, I expect you to change to suit me."	"I expect you to listen to and respect my opinion, and then share your opinions with me in return."
"I will win and you will lose."	"We both win."

1. Both partners are healthy and independent, and neither attempts to control the other.
2. One partner is a controller; the other is a submitter.
3. Both partners are controllers (this relationship doesn't last very long).

When two controllers are in a relationship together, the result is pure turmoil! Their partnership—if you can call it that—is characterized by the pursuit of vengeance as a means to achieve victory. Score keeping—who's on top—is an ongoing ritual. The entire focus in a two-controller relationship is: "Who is winning?" You are either winning or you are losing. No middle ground exists.

This is the worst type of codependency. Both partners are locked in a covert agreement to control one another—by blackmail if necessary. The missiles are continually launched back and forth across the enemy lines.

Partners in a two-controller relationship believe the high drama is exciting, even sexually stimulating. Indeed, the highs and lows of such turmoil can be addictive, much like the highs and lows of compulsive gambling or drug use. When the couple is experiencing a low, they know one thing for certain: they can only go up from there. This type of relationship tears down the partners, ripping away what little self-esteem they have.

Unlike people in a healthy relationship, which promotes personal growth, two controllers won't see much growth in their relationship.

In any dysfunctional relationship, control and dependency are the central unhealthy issues. Sometimes, it's difficult to know for sure if you are a controlling person, or if your partner is a controlling person. The controlling roles can even switch or change within the same relationship, according to the issues. It's easy to identify controlling behavior in other couples, but it's hard to be objective when it's your own relationship.

Signs of Controlling Behavior

The following questions will help you identify whether or not you are behaving in a controlling manner.

1. Do I always need to be right?
2. Do I always think my ideas are best?
3. Do I feel good, or powerful, when I get someone else to do something for me?
4. Do I issue demands because I need to validate that I'm in charge?
5. Do I feel a need to get revenge, get even, or get back at people?

If you answered "yes" to at least two questions, you are acting as a controlling person. This is not a put-down; this is a way of understanding which behaviors are interfering with your experiencing a healthy, fulfilling relationship. If you feel lonely in your present partnership, controlling behavior is one reason. Once you know the reason for a problem, the solution is not far away.

Remember, your behavior is not you. If you see that you have a habit that creates problems, don't jump to the conclusion that you're not lovable, or that everybody's unfriendly; first examine your own behavior. Take an honest inventory of your behavior and decide to change the defeating behavior to productive behavior.

Beneath the behavior of controllers lie fear and low self-esteem. Controllers fear rejection and abandonment; they cannot imagine that anyone would love them for themselves. "The only way to have a relationship is by forcing my partner constantly to prove her love to me"— this is one of the controller's underlying beliefs.

Mental health comes from high self-esteem, and high

97

self-esteem comes from treating yourself and others with respect. As you clarify what your wants are, and as you take steps toward fulfilling those wants, your desire to control others will naturally lessen.

Are you being controlled?

What if you are not the controller in the relationship, but instead suspect that you are being controlled? What if you suspect you are the submissive person in a dysfunctional relationship?

Below are some questions to help you identify whether you are being controlled. As always, honest answers provide the most useful information.

1. Do I feel insecure?
2. Do I feel unimportant?
3. Do I feel forced to behave against my wishes or better judgment?
4. Do I feel overwhelmed, or fear I have no choices or options?
5. Do I feel worthless?
6. Do I fear abandonment, or rejection, or that my partner will harm me, either physically or emotionally?
7. Do I feel doubtful, as if I can't make a decision?
8. Do I feel anxious as though I need to be with my partner to feel secure, whether for money, love, safety, or security?

Being controlled is not only dangerous to your self-esteem, it can be deadly. Each year, more than fourteen hundred women are killed at the hands of their boyfriends or husbands. The temper of a controller can be lethal!

Controlling people become more abusive when they feel their victims aren't complying. They may get physically abusive if they feel they are losing control over you. ("I told you that you could go to school one night a week, damn it! Not two nights a week!")

The cycles a controlling relationship often follows ensures that the codependent person will stay hooked. First, the controller forces or bullies to get control, and then may placate or rescue the dependent partner, which rewards the victim for staying with the controller.

For example, Joel would scream at Melinda, intimidating her to comply with his requests. Melinda would give in, but she would cry and exhibit her unhappiness. He would fear losing her, so he'd give her a gift the next day. He would also apologize. When Joel is "nice," Melinda would believe that he had finally changed into the man of her dreams. "He's perfect on days he's sorry for screaming at me," Melinda says. "I keep thinking that one day he'll stop screaming, and he'll just be a nice guy all of the time."

Codependents like Melinda try to convince themselves they are in love with the controller. But it is impossible to love someone who abuses you, unless you are in love with abuse.

What Should I Do about This?

If you are in a controlling relationship, you'll need to take steps to help yourself. Waiting for your controlling partner to change, without the help of therapy, is futile. If you know what you want, and you know you don't want a dysfunctional relationship, you owe it to yourself to take these steps.

The first step is recognizing that you're emotionally unhealthy, or you would never have allowed this dysfunctional relationship to occur in the first place.

The second step is understanding why you are emotionally unhealthy. You are responsible for having continued in the abusive relationship. There is a reason why you didn't put a stop to it sooner. Perhaps you doubt yourself, or are accustomed to receiving abuse, something you probably learned in childhood. Perhaps you fear rejection or abandonment.

When you allow someone to abuse or control you, it is actually self-abuse. Why would you do something like that to yourself? It is a dysfunctional relationship called enmeshment, where you are meeting other's needs and wants, but not your own.

Self-abuse is not taking care of yourself. If you are living a life you don't want to live, it's important to ask yourself why. It is an extremely difficult cycle to break without help If you are not emotionally healthy, you are not prepared to confront an abusive situation. If you are in a physically or emotionally abusive situation, you need to seek professional help from a domestic violence shelter or a therapist.

I know it's difficult. You already suffer from shame and low self-esteem, and the idea of getting help may make you feel even weaker. But focus on the benefits of getting help. You can only go up from here. You don't need, and shouldn't ask for, the abuser's permission before you seek professional help. Do it for yourself as a good first step toward getting the fulfilling life you deserve.

Learn from your abusive relationship, so you'll avoid getting into another one in the future. Too many women leave one abuser, and go right into the arms of another.

Learn to accept people for who they are, and stop falling in love with a person's potential, unless—and this is a big unless—you see that person making real effort and progress toward growth and improvement. If you are growing, and your partner is stagnating, you will grow apart.

Sharing Your Wants versus Controlling

In a healthy relationship, both partners teach one another what they want. Healthy people take sole responsibility for teaching their partners about their boundaries, and understanding their partner's boundaries. Both partners can *choose* to respond in accordance with their own boundaries, or not. The choice belong to each of them. On the other hand, if one partner tells the other to adhere to his or her boundaries, that is controlling behavior.

Debbie and Mark have been dating one another exclusively for one year; they are discussing marriage. Debbie is reluctant to marry Mark, however, because of his continued involvement with an ex-girlfriend. Mark argues that, as long as he is not having sex with his ex-girlfriend, there should be no problem with his sharing meals with her. Debbie sees it differently, and feels strongly that she can not accept Mark's continued involvement with a person he once slept with.

In a healthy relationship, Debbie would share her concerns and feelings with Mark. She would be able to say, "Here is how I feel. I am not telling you what to do, Mark. You choose whether or not to continue seeing your ex-girlfriend." Mark, then, would be free to make his choice. Debbie would also be free to either continue or end the relationship if Mark continued to see his ex-girlfriend.

In an unhealthy relationship; Debbie would demand that Mark stop seeing his ex-girlfriend. She would give him an ultimatum. This type of behavior, of course, never yields a positive result. In this case, Mark would probably either break up with Debbie, or start hiding his ongoing relationship with his ex-girlfriend.

Holding rather than sharing feelings with a partner, and then exploding into a rage every few months is a common destructive pattern. Lucille was upset that her husband, Roger, wouldn't call when he was coming home late from work. But rather than confront Roger, Lucille would pretend that everything was fine. Consequently Roger was always shocked when Lucille would blow up at him and scream, "You are a thought-less and uncaring jerk!"

Was Lucille justified in being upset at Roger for not calling when he'd be late? Absolutely. Was Lucille play-ing fairly by not revealing her hurt feelings to Roger? Absolutely not.

Everyone should have boundaries. It's not a sign of weakness. In fact, boundaries are the hallmark of health and strength. People with poor boundaries have low self-esteem; some clinicians label such individuals as having a borderline personality disorder. That diagnosis is simply a fancy way of saying: the client has a poor understanding and self-respect of her boundaries. As a result, her relationships with herself and others are chaotic and painful.

Getting What You Want, in a Healthy Way

Any time a people think they have the right to control

another person, they are taking on the role of the parent in the relationship. They are assuming they know what is right or wrong. But in a relationship, there really is no absolute right or wrong, except for moral and legal issues involving honesty and fairness.

People control, or are dependent, because they believe that is the only way to get what they want. They've never been shown an alternative. In actuality, there is only one way to get what you want: by being crystal clear about what you want, and then taking the steps to attain it.

You *can* have what you want: you can have the relationship you want. You can have the mate with the qualities you want (as long as your expectations are in line with reality). It will take some work. As I said at the beginning of the book, your quest will be difficult and uncomfortable. But it does work, and the results are worth it. It's like any worthwhile goal—getting physically fit, for example—getting the love that you want takes deliberate planning and effort. Goals are not attained by accident.

Love fulfillment doesn't involve a power struggle. Relationships blossom when partners stop trying to control each other and start taking responsibility for their own actions.

NEGOTIATING FOR LOVE

Once both partners agree that a problem exists, the next step is to figure out what to do about it. The most direct means to solving any problem is negotiation. Negotiation is simply the process of defining problems and creating mutually beneficial solutions.

Those familiar with business negotiation may not have considered negotiation as an option in a love relationship. But there are many parallels between the two. The art of negotiating business strategies is applicable to the resolution of relationship differences. Negotiating for a win-win result is the objective regardless of whether the two people are married or in business together.

Negotiating to solve problems maintains a couple's unity. When couples can't, or won't, negotiate, the relationship deteriorates rapidly. Two people who refuse to work together on solving problems are incompatible, and shouldn't be in a relationship. There really is no other healthy choice but to negotiate when disagreements or problems inevitably arise.

The three basic ingredients of negotiating within relationships are as follows:

1. Both people must have the same goal: a harmonious, loving relationship.
2. Both people must agree to focus on the problem or issue, and not focus on blaming one another.
3. Both people must agree to drop their defenses and let go of the need to be right.

What Is Negotiation?

Because negotiating in a love relationship may be a novel concept, let's start by defining what we're talking about. For our purposes, negotiation consists of three separate components: First, negotiation involves bringing a confronting issue to your partner. A confronting issue is something that's uncomfortable to talk about, yet something that needs to be resolved. Second, the confronting issue involves both partners, and both partners are motivated to do something to resolve the confronting issue. And third, both partners must listen to one another's response for negotiation to occur.

The partner who brings up the confronting issue must be prepared to do some research, or back up their contention. Without prior research, negotiation may be thwarted until more information is gathered.

Sandy wants to replace her kitchen cabinets. The project will affect both her and her husband, Ralph, in terms of cost and inconvenience. Sandy is therefore responsible for negotiating this want with Ralph. But before Ralph can have an intelligent, informed discussion about kitchen cabinet replacements, both partners need some information.

Because the want of kitchen cabinets is Sandy's, she is responsible for researching the project. So, she gets estimates, investigates the types and prices of cabinets available, and checks a few contractor references. She is now ready to negotiate with Ralph.

Before you bring an issue to the table, you should be clear about the nature of the problem. Bringing up general complaints is just too vague for any sort of resolution to occur.

Below are some general guidelines to ensure smoother, more successful, negotiations with your partner.

- First, ask yourself, "What is the real problem here? What I am really upset about?" Have a very clear idea in your mind before addressing your partner. Once you've defined a problem clearly, you're halfway there to solving it.
- Next, present the problem to your partner in a direct, positive way. Avoid hostility, either in your vocabulary, tone of voice, or body language. If frightened or distracted by your hostility, your partner won't be able to hear your message.
- Once you've presented the problem, keep the discussion focused on the issue rather than on each other. Do not get sidetracked into a blaming match; this is neither productive, nor healthy. Instead, try to be open to the scenarios that may occur in response to your bringing up a confronting issue: Your partner may either leave, or ask you to leave. Your partner may want to have a conflict. Your partner may want to have a discussion. (You may not like some of these scenarios, but they may occur nonetheless.)

It is perfectly okay for you and your partner to disagree—even the most happily married couples don't see
eye to eye on everything. The issue isn't that you disagree, but rather how you deal with the disagreement.

Couples who fight differ from couples who argue.
It's important to understand the difference. Arguing is
healthy and constructive, fighting is not. I define arguing
as the exchange of opinions, a discussion. It provides an
opportunity to state your views and listen to the views
of your partner. After all, how can a problem be solved
if both sides don't express their opinions? Fighting
means to be in conflict. It's negative and destructive.
While fighting occurs, there is hostility. No one listens.
While arguing, however, there is communication. The
arguing couple is committed to finding a solution: "We
both win." The fighting couple focuses only on wining:
"I win, you lose."

Now, an argument may be heated. That's okay, as
long as both partners treat each other with courtesy and
respect. The outcome of a fight, on the other hand, is
certain to be unsatisfactory because a mutually beneficial
solution is excluded. An argument where both sides
abide by the rules is the first step toward resolution and
harmony. Learn and practice the techniques of arguing,
and eliminate fighting. There's a big difference between
the two!

Arguing—not fighting—is positive for couples; arguments force both partners to look for solutions. Their
mutual focus is on finding solutions that will benefit the
couple, rather than each partner trying to win at the
expense of the other. Arguing leads to win-win solutions; fighting leads to win-lose outcomes.

Most of us have been in a conflict that we won.
Maybe we yelled louder, or threw our weight around in

Arguing	**Fighting**
"I disagree with you."	"You are wrong; I am right."
"We'll see things differently from time to time. That's okay, it's normal for two people to disagree."	"I want us to always agree, and the easiest way is if you'll just agree with my ideas."
"I'm presenting my viewpoints, and will listen to your opinions, as well."	"I'm right, so my opinion is the only one that counts."
"Let's look for mutually beneficial solutions so we can resolve this."	"I need to win, or I'm the loser. My solution is the only solution"
"Let's discuss the issues rationally and calmly."	"I can scream louder and longer than you can."
"We are equals."	"I'm the boss."

a manipulative or unfair way. But the victory we win in such instances is hollow, it never feels good for long. The loser is filled with resentment and vengeance and will look for ways to get even. The victory is temporary; it's simply a prelude to more fights.

Winning through an argument feels good, however, because both parties benefit from the solution. In negotiation, no one loses, suffers or sacrifices. Each partner modifies rather than abandons their wants.

When Alan and Betty were dating, they discussed

having a baby together. Now, three years into their marriage, Betty really wants a child but Alan has changed his stance. He tells Betty, "I don't think I'm ready to be a father."

Betty has several choices, and it's up to her to decide which will ultimately fulfill her wants.

- Betty can attempt to pretend, to herself and to Alan, that it really doesn't matter whether or not she has a baby.
- Betty can genuinely decide she doesn't want to have a baby, that being with Alan is her greater want.
- Betty can tell Alan how important having a baby is to her, and try to negotiate with him. If he won't negotiate, the couple is not compatible. If he decides he doesn't want a baby, Betty has to decide for herself what to do: If her greater want is to have a baby, she will have to leave Alan and either be a single mother, or be with a man who wants a baby.
- Betty can negotiate with Alan. If he genuinely decides he wants a baby, the issue is solved.

Facing a Problem, in the Name of Love

An old adage says, "It's easy to have a great marriage. Just always remember to say those three magical words: 'Honey, You're Right.'" Caving in to another person's opinions and wishes rarely works in real life, however.

In fact, caving in can create further conflict. When Andrea said, "I would like to discuss our retirement plans," Jim replied, "I don't want to talk about that. End of discussion!"

What Jim was saying to Andrea, essentially, was: "Your opinions and feelings don't matter to me." No wonder Andrea felt demoralized and hurt by Jim's unwillingness to discuss this important issue with her.

Sometimes, couples are reluctant to negotiate, for fear of uncovering areas of disagreement. There's a deep yearning for a problem-free relationship, where both partners see eye to eye about everything. Yet, such a relationship is unrealistic. Furthermore, if the couples don't negotiate, the relationship will end up being anything but problem-free.

If you don't communicate your complaints to your partner, there's no reason for that person to believe you're anything but satisfied. And, why should your partner change if they believe you are satisfied?

Smart couples risk the discovery of areas of disagreement within their relationship. They detach from the need to be right, or the need to score victories at the expense of their partners, and instead focus their energies and time working toward on compatible solutions.

Negotiating Guidelines

Negotiation is a structured way to examine problems and look for solutions. Conflict is completely unstructured, and that lack of structure is one reason why fights are unproductive.

Negotiating guidelines, strategies, and structures have been developed over the years by business leaders, foreign affairs negotiators, industrial psychologists, and other experts. I've borrowed this knowledge—born of the work world—and adapted it to relationships.

Business negotiators understand the value of following time-honored structures and guidelines when negotiating solutions. The following guidelines will help couples minimize needless fighting, and maximize intelligent discussions.

- Approach your partner intelligently. You know him or her well enough to anticipate and predict possible reactions. Do both of you a favor and avoid saying phrases or acting in a way that you *know* push buttons or trigger anger. For example, if you know your husband hates to be corrected, it would be self-destructive to say, "Brad, you are wrong. The right way is . . ."
- Offer several alternative solutions during negotiation. Say, "My preference would be to have access to the car all day long. But because you need to use the car, also, here are some other options that may work.
- Be flexible, in order to find a solution. Don't hold onto one, favorite solution, to the exclusion of all others. Inflexibility is a form of a power struggle for control, and that is dysfunctional.
- Keep the focus on finding a solution, not on finding whom to blame.
- Make sure the solutions you offer are: realistic, attainable, and understandable.
- Present your solution calmly. Avoid acting like you are obsessed with your idea. Also avoid demanding that your partner agree with your solution. Nobody likes to be told what to do, and your partner reject your solution to rebel—even if the solution is in your partner's best interests.
- Help your partner visualize your solution by painting a verbal picture of what you're offering.

112

The Four Steps of Negotiations

1. *Confront.* Present your issue. This may mean communicating your wants to your partner or confronting your partner about unacceptable behavior (asserting your boundaries). Confronting is the action of spelling out your wants and/or boundaries directly. It does not mean being aggressive, controlling, or hostile."

2. *Argue.* Both partners present their feelings and thoughts about the issue. It's important not to confuse the term *argue* with *fight.* As with confronting, arguing does not involve controlling or hostile behavior.

3. *Negotiate.* The partners interact and brainstorm, both focusing on the common goal of coming up with a win-win solution. Healthy negotiation hinges upon cooperation and communication, not gaming or manipulation.

4. *Solution.* A healthy solution benefits both partners. They should each find increased self-esteem and have their wants fulfilled.

Anything else, or any other outcome,
signals an incompatible couple.

The most viable solutions are those that are easy to implement, and easy to attain. Solutions that are time-consuming to adopt might be ignored or procrastinated—which leaves you with no solution.

- Don't impose artificial time constraints on finding a solution; your negotiation may require more than one session. The fact that partners enter into a discussion does not mean that there has to be an arbitrary time limit for resolving the problem. Sometimes, it's simply not possible to solve a problem in one day. If you do decide to continue the negotiation at a future time, be sure to set a firm appointment for reconvening.

Ground rules to negotiating

If both partners are truly interested in finding a solution, they'll want to make the negotiation process as smooth and as productive as possible. The goal of negotiating is presenting an issue, listening to your partner, and brainstorming possible solutions; it is not to get revenge, extract an apology, or label one person as bad. Keep the discussion focused on the issues.

Assuming, then, that both partners want to find a resolution, the following do's and don'ts lend themselves to successful negotiation.

Do: Negotiate in an appropriate place.
Don't: Negotiate in the bedroom. This room needs to be an oasis free of any anger or tension that could contaminate it. Choose an emotionally neutral location, such as the kitchen or living room.
Don't: Negotiate in one partner's office or den. In other words, don't negotiate in a room that belongs to one partner; the other partner will feel disadvantaged.
Don't: Negotiate while driving a car, especially if defiant (destructive, aggressive) anger is probable. It's too dangerous and too risky!
Do: Choose an appropriate time for negotiation.
Don't: Try to negotiate with a partner who is about to walk out the door to go to work or school.

Do: Set an appointment to negotiate.

Don't: Try to negotiate when you are with other people. An audience will distract both partners away from finding a solution.

Don't: Demand that your partner drop everything and negotiate right this instant. Such a demand adds extra tension to the situation.

Strategies to help you negotiate successfully

The way you present your issue can mean the difference between a successful negotiation and a disastrous fight. You can set the tone for a mature, productive discussion by choosing your words carefully. This doesn't mean you should placate or talk down to your partner. It simply means you should convey your meaning in a way that your partner can hear what you are really saying.

Below are some strategies to help get your points across:

- First, help your partner feel safe. It's natural for your partner to be a little tense and fearful, worrying for example, "What is she upset about? Did I do something wrong?" Put your partner at ease; help him drop his defenses by first offering sincere praise. A little compliment, such as, "Honey, I really appreciate how you're so open and willing to listen to me," goes a long way toward opening his ears and his mind to what you're about to say.

- State your issue with the built-in assumption that you both are friends, not enemies. You can soften your statement without watering down your message. For example; "I know you didn't mean to hurt my feelings, but here's how I perceived your behavior yesterday." Certainly, a statement like that is preferable to this: "You don't care about anybody's feelings but your own!"

- Begin with an *I* statement rather than a *you* statement. Better to say "I felt angry when you . . ." than "You made me angry when you . . ." In the first statement, your partner will be able to listen to you; in the second, your partner will be too defensive to listen to you. You have a right to your feelings. Own them. Expressing your feelings constructively, rather than attacking your partner, will help you to arrive at a solution. Always remember, the ultimate goal of negotiation is not to blame but to solve.

- Stay focused on the issue. Don't get sidetracked into topics that aren't directly relevant to finding a solution. Avoid discussing events from the past ("What about two years ago, when you stayed out all night with your friends and didn't call me?"), blaming ("Are you saying it's my fault the car ran out of gas?"), or tangents ("Well, this reminds me of the time you forgot my birthday!").

- Listen to your partner with your eyes and your body, as well as with your ears. If your partner thinks you are not listening, she is likely to become upset. Convey your interest in her opinion by maintaining appropriate eye contact and leaning toward her. Looking at your partner also helps you negotiate more effectively: your partner's body language yields valuable information about her opinions and reactions to the issue being discussed. She may be saying one thing, but really feeling quite the opposite. Her body

116

language can help you understand her true stance on the matter.

- Acknowledge that you've heard your partner. Paraphrasing what you heard, such as, "So, what you are saying is (summarize your understanding of your partner's statement)," will go a long way toward ensuring accurate interaction. Your partner will know he's been heard, and will have the opportunity to correct any misunderstandings. These comments don't necessarily mean that you agree with your partner, just that you've understood his position.

Diffusing Heated Discussions

Tempers flair when opinions differ. Love relationships, which are based on strong emotions in the first place, are ripe environments for heated arguments.

There are basically two ways in which people interact and converse: they share opinions and they share facts. Neither should produce conflict. Everyone has the right to their opinions. Why should anyone fight about an agreed-upon fact? The principle reason people get into conflict is a need to win. They stubbornly hold onto the belief, "I'm right and you're wrong. My way is the best way; if you don't do it my way, you are stupid!"

No one should accept verbal abuse from a partner. But during those times when a partner becomes upset during negotiations (as long as he or she isn't behaving abusively), the following phrases diffuse the heat: (Choose whichever most accurately reflects your true feelings.)

Phrases That Diffuse Heated Negotiations

"I guess you are yelling because you want to make sure I hear your point."

"I feel uncomfortable dealing with this subject when you're so obviously upset. Could we discuss this later today (suggest a time)?"

"What do you think the outcome would be if we tried things your way?"

"What solutions are you willing to consider, and which are totally unacceptable to you?"

"What parts of this issue are most important to you?"

"I hear you saying there are no other possible solutions to this problem."

Negotiating Styles

In addition to strategies, there are different negotiating styles. Whether for business or for love, negotiating successfully requires understanding the other person's personality and interests. In love negotiation, it is vital.

Consider your partner's style when negotiating.

Is he pragmatic and practical? He'll more likely respond to black-and-white facts than to emotional complaints.

118

Is she more visual than auditory? Then she'll more likely respond to a sketch or a vivid description, than words.

Is he the detail-oriented, engineer type? Then he will respect, and be more interested in, your statements, if they are thoroughly explained, with all the details included. This type of person will ask a lot of questions, because he wants to understand all of the details.

Is she the nurturing, mothering type? She will be more focused on maintaining the harmony of the relationship than on finding a solution to the problem. Stay on track with this type of person; ultimately the solution is what will keep your relationship nurturing for both of you.

Negotiating styles often differ between men and women. In general, men concentrate on winning and problem solving, while women focus on creating and maintaining relationships and intimacy. Styles are neither good nor bad, they just are. The important point is to stay aware of the ways in which your partner views the world and takes in new information. This isn't manipulation; it's communication based on your understanding of your partner's style.

Solution Strategies

Once you and your partner agree on a solution, you each must clearly spell out your understanding of your responsibility in carrying out the solution. It's not enough to assume that both you and your partner will just know what needs to be done. Instead, clearly divide duties, or choose tasks. That way, you will understand what is expected of you, and what is expected of your partner.

Does your intuition give you any indication of whether or not your partner will follow through on his or her end of the solution? If you have doubts—based on past performance or on your intuition—communicate your concern. For example: "I am expecting you to honor this agreement." Or, "I need to know from you: are you going to live up to this agreement?"

Some couples resolve this problem by writing out their agreements, and then posting their expectations in view, such as on the refrigerator or a bathroom mirror. Tape-recording or video taping your discussion is another alternative.

Relying solely on the memories of two people who have different interests is not always the best idea. You're likely to have very different memories of your discussion, and the agreed-upon solution. Why set yourself up for future conflict? It's so much easier to spell everything in the first place in writing or on tape.

By this time, all of this talk about negotiation may seem unattainable, unrealistic, and too much trouble. Remember, some people opt for an easier way out when they find out that self-fulfillment involves effort. Please keep in mind: the rewards are definitely worth your effort.

Remember, too: the other option is to be controlled, endure conflict and to lose your self-respect. But, that's not really an option, is it?

BOUNDARIES AND THE SANDBOX

Being part of a couple doesn't mean you must sacrifice your individuality. As we've seen, accepting responsibility for your own happiness, needs, and wants helps any couple's unity. Conversely, neither unity nor the union will last long if one or both partners feel dissatisfied with their lives.

There's a popular, but unhealthy, notion about romance—namely, that two people in love should fuse together as one, or that when two people who are missing something join, they become whole and complete. Romance novels perpetuate the belief that a love partner should be able to read our minds, or know automatically what we want.

A healthy relationship is not a fusion of two people into one. Rather, it requires a healthy respect for the individuality of each partner. Two whole, healthy, complete partners come together to make a whole, healthy, complete relationship.

Unhealthy Romance and Love Beliefs	Healthy Romance and Love Beliefs
"We will unite and become one."	"We are two separate individuals who will grow, side by side."
"Each of us is missing something and is incomplete, but our love will fill the gaps in ourselves, and in our lives."	"The relationship will be a growth experience for both of us, but we won't burden our love by expecting it to be our sole source of fulfillment."
"I expect my partner to know what my needs and wants are, and then take action to fulfill them for me."	"I expect you, my partner, to act responsibly in meeting your own needs and wants. I invite you to share them with me, and I will encourage your efforts to attain them."
"If I'm unhappy, it's my partner's fault; I'll have no choice but to get a new partner."	"If I'm unhappy, I'll first look to myself to see what needs I'm not meeting for myself."

How We Learn about Boundaries

Around each of us, whether we are in a relationship or not, lies a boundary separating us from other people.

This boundary is our means of protecting ourselves from inappropriate behavior. It is like a fence around our property—a fence that we can choose to open for others, or keep closed.

The following are examples of boundaries.

- "I want one hour alone a night, without interruption, to complete my school work."
- "I want to go to aerobics class five times a week."
- "I want to watch football on television, uninterrupted."
- "I want to go out with my friends one night a week."
- "I will not accept abuse, either physical or emotional."
- "I will not accept infidelity. If you cheat on me, I leave."
- "I will not accept dishonesty and deception. I expect you to be above-board with me at all times."
- "We are sharing a joint checking account. I expect you to be responsible about recording your purchases, so we will always know what our account balance is."
- "I expect you to consult me before making a purchase that involves my money or will affect my lifestyle."
- "I expect you to consult me before making plans that involve me."

During early childhood, we are not aware of our separateness from others. It's normal for a child to feel fused with his mother. Adolescence is marked by the painful,

123

but necessary, step of realizing our separateness from our parents. We call separation-individuation, the process of growing up and out.

During adolescence, teenagers rebel against their parents and instinctively seek to provide their own needs and wants. They want to buy their own food and their own clothes. They want their own transportation and the ability to come and go as they please. This painful power struggle challenges even the most experienced and patient of parents, as teenagers awkwardly seek independence. The pain comes from the adolescent having one foot in childhood, and the other in adulthood. The adolescent is still dependent on his parents, but doesn't want to be.

In healthy families, parents insist on adolescents taking appropriate responsibility for themselves. As a result, they learn to respect themselves and their responsibilities, such as doing homework, maintaining an after-school job, feeding the dog, taking care of personal hygiene, and performing household chores.

In dysfunctional families, parents feel threatened as their children begin to grow away from them. They demonstrate a lack of trust and respect for their children's undertakings. If, for example, a mother has invested her identity and self-worth in her youngster, she may try to prevent the separation-individuation process from occurring. "I'm not ready for him to grow up yet," "I'll feel unwanted and empty if my child is no longer dependent on me," "If I admit that my child is all grown up, I must admit I've grown older, too"—these are the fears of parents who block their children's separation process.

Children who are abused—either sexually, emotionally, or physically—are forced to relinquish their boundaries. The abused child learns; "My body doesn't belong to me. Others can take my body and abuse it." Since the abuser is often the child's parent or another person who symbolizes love, the child's undeveloped boundaries carry over into their adult love relationships. Abuse survivors learn to expect mistreatment from a love partner, because their earliest experiences mix love with abuse.

Boundaries as Adults

We all have personal values we don't allow others to violate or encroach upon. Emotionally healthy people guard these values behind a perimeter, or boundary. People with poor boundaries fear, "I must conform to my partner's expectations, or my partner will leave me, or I am not a good person."

An important part of a healthy adult relationship is the setting up, and the maintenance of, our personal boundaries. Often, a boundary is confused with a wall. But I'm not talking about putting up a wall that blocks out emotional intimacy. Set the boundary threshold at a level allowing observation and evaluation of your surroundings. Boundaries and intimacy walls are entirely different, as spelled out on page 126.

Healthy people don't have walls that separate them from other people; rather, they have boundaries. A boundary is more like a picket fence than a wall; a healthy boundary is of a height that allows connections with the outside world, but still affords protection. Similarly, boundaries that are either too high (which result in isolation) or too low (which results in intrusiveness and abusiveness) are unhealthy.

A big difference between walls and boundaries is

A Wall	A Boundary
isolates people from one another; they don't know or really understand one another	allows partners to coexist harmoniously, because they know is expected of them
comes from self-doubt: "I don't want you to know the real me."	comes from self-respect: "Here's what I'll accept, and what I won't accept."
is dishonest and deceptive; "I'll pretend to be happy, so you won't reject me. But I may leave you because you're not treating me the way I secretly want you to treat me."	is honest and forthright: "I will spell out for you exactly what treatment I won't accept, I will let you know if you are violating my boundaries, and I will expect you to honor them."
is rigid and unyielding.	is flexible, when appropriate

flexibility. The image of a fence that has a gate attached to it paints the picture of a flexible boundary. When the owner wants others to come in, the gate allows access. Walls, which are built on a premise of fear and defensiveness, have no gates—nobody is allowed in, ever.

For example, Teresa has set a boundary with her boyfriend, Todd, that she needs twenty-four hours notice before a date. Teresa refuses to go on a last-minute date, simply because Todd failed to plan and ask her out ahead of time. Teresa's boundary protects her from last-minute scrambling, and wondering what she will be doing on Friday night. In this way, her boundary affords both peace of mind and self-respect.

Teresa also has the right to flex her boundary when she wants to. Todd respects her boundary, and usually asks her out several days in advance of his planned dates. One night, however, he got backstage passes at the last-minute to see their favorite music group. In this instance, Teresa would certainly adjust her twenty-four-hour-notice rule.

Instead, if her rule were a wall, Teresa would be rigid and inflexible. And she wouldn't get to go back-stage to see her favorite band. Because Teresa is healthy enough to know the difference between a last-minute opportunity and an instance when someone is trying to use her, she agreed to accompany Todd.

A flexible boundary says; "There's a gate on my boundary with a latch accessible only to me. There will be people I meet for whom I choose to open the gate, people I choose to invite into my life. Ultimately, it's my choice."

Inherent with spelling out your boundaries to another person is the risk that they won't agree to your terms. They may disagree with you or reject you. The most important relationship is the relationship you have with yourself. A person who honestly discloses—and maintains—personal boundaries to a partner in essence is saying, "I want you to like me, but I love myself enough to risk that you may not. I may set boundaries, but there's room to negotiate and there is a gate."

Men are typically better at setting boundaries than women. They rarely think twice about saying, "No I can't go with you; there's a football game on television I want to watch."

Why? Perhaps it is because men are taught that they come first, while women are taught to take care of others. Women learn to worry about whether people are happy and getting along; they become peacemakers. Sometimes, however, these good intentions lead women to become people pleasers, an unhealthy image that eventually lowers their own self-esteem.

Women who learn to establish and maintain their boundaries are much happier with themselves and their relationship, than women who allow their partners to control them. It's a choice we all have to make. Those who are fortunate learn how to establish and express their boundaries in childhood. The rest of us learn as adults.

Boundaries and Relationships

When you live with another person, your boundaries overlap and cross with that person's. This necessitates negotiation. For example, Kate wanted to run the dishwasher right after dinner because it was convenient for her. Her husband, Ed, objected saying, "The dishwasher is too noisy when I'm trying to watch television." The couple must negotiate their boundaries and create a mutual solution—something that enables both of them to win.

In this instance, Ed agreed to take responsibility for turning on the dishwasher right before he went to bed at night. Both Kate and Ed were pleased with the solution.

Having boundaries that outline your wants and expectations, and having the ability to negotiate those boundaries, are important parts of having a fulfilling relationship. You set boundaries in order to take care of yourself, not to manipulate or to create power struggles. You must set limits that you are willing to protect and to maintain.

Some boundaries are necessarily more rigid than others. For instance, you decide that you will not, under any circumstances, accept extramarital affairs, physical abuse, or unhealthy behavior. Other boundaries, however, are flexible, when you decide you want to flex them.

Of course, boundaries are worthless unless other people know about them. As we've seen, it's unhealthy to stew silently about another person violating your boundaries. How is anyone supposed to know your limits unless you communicate them?

Most people wait until after a boundary has been crossed in a relationship before they say anything. Ideally, you should tell your partner what your boundaries are in the beginning of a relationship. But when a relationship is new, it may not feel very romantic to bring up something seemingly negative. Keep in mind: anger and resentment are the great killers of romance. If you tell your partner your boundaries from the outset, you're less apt to feel unresolved anger or resentment toward your partner later on. You've been upfront and fair by telling your partner what your rules consist of. Now, you can be hopeful that your partner will respect the rules. If not, self-respect demands that you take action.

Everyone has boundaries, and that every relationship will involve boundary violation, from time to time. The important distinction between healthy and unhealthy relationships lies in how the partners deal with boundary violations.

Declaring your boundaries to your partner shouldn't involve threatening, bluffing, or moralizing. These are unnecessary, destructive, and unhealthy. Rose didn't like it when her boyfriend, Bill, called her a bitch. It violated her boundaries about name-calling, and not allowing anyone to treat her in a way that compromised her integrity or self-esteem.

Rose had two choices: she could ignore Bill's name-calling, which would result in Bill assuming that Rose didn't mind his calling her a bitch. Or she could confront Bill's behavior. The second, of course, is the only healthy choice. But it would be neither healthy nor productive for Rose to say, "Bill, you damn bastard! How dare you call me a bitch!" Tit for tat is not a part of a healthy, functional relationship.

Being a healthy person, Rose chose option number two. Her purpose was not retaliation, but instruction. She had never told Bill about her boundary. So she told him when he crossed it: "Bill, I don't accept being called a bitch or any other derogatory name, for that matter." Had he not accepted Rose's boundary, she would have taken care of herself by leaving the relationship.

Rose explained Bill's options to him. The solution is a change in his behavior. As an adult, Bill can now make his own choices, because he now knows the consequences. As long as Rose behaves responsibly toward herself, and adheres to the boundary conditions she has spelled out, Bill will respect her and Rose will respect herself. The lines of responsibility are clearly defined. If Bill does not respect Rose's boundary, then he must accept total responsibility for the problem, and, for the eventual dissolution of the relationship. If Bill chooses not to change, it will signal certain incompatibility for this couple.

When others cross our boundaries—by mistreating us, betraying us, belittling us, or doing something we won't tolerate—the healthy person responds with action. This is functional. It is the unhealthy person that takes other action, aggressive or passive, in its form.

As we've learned, boundary violations are inevitable in a relationship. Because these boundary violations result in disharmony, it is essential to know what your boundaries are. Without mutual understanding of one another's boundaries, there will be no clear understanding of the reasons for discord. And because no problem can be solved until it is defined, the dissatisfaction will persist.

Many people feel confused about their own boundaries. Maybe they've never taken the time to spell out what they want and don't want. Perhaps they've adopted another person's wants—a parent's or a spouse's—for example, "Well, these are the things I should want," they think. Yet, the only wants and boundaries that matter are those that are genuine, those that belong to you. The key is to be 100 percent honest with yourself when deciding what you want.

Below are questions to help you in defining your boundaries. Probably, you already know what you will and won't accept in a relationship. Answering these questions will help you clarify those wants, and, perhaps add to them. While answering them, allow yourself to admit what you truly want. Remember: don't let other people define your wants or you. Only you can do that.

1. What behaviors from others are absolutely unacceptable to me?
2. What behaviors from others irritate or upset me?
3. What do I expect from my partner?

131

4. What leisure activities are important to me?
5. What habits (sleeping, eating, vacationing, and so on) are important to my overall peace of mind?
6. What is my role or responsibility in my relationship?
7. What are my responsibilities to myself, to ensure my needs are met?
8. What are my responsibilities to myself, to ensure that my wants are met?
9. To what priorities and values must I adhere, in order to maintain my integrity?

As you ponder these questions, you may want to write notes about the answers that materialize. These form the basis of your boundaries, and they are important to share with your partner.

Discerning between Healthy and Unhealthy Boundaries

Signs of Healthy Boundaries:

-   knowing what you expect from others
-   taking action to let others know what your boundaries are
-   asking consistent action to protect your boundaries
-   they are of a height that allows you to observe your surroundings
-   respecting your own right to privacy

Signs of Unhealthy Boundaries:

- not knowing, or feeling confused, about how you want to be treated
- not communicating what you want, and what you won't accept
- allowing others to use or abuse you without confronting them
- They are of a height that isolates you from others
- feeling compelled to tell all

The last sign in each category stresses an important point: You have the right to your private thoughts and feelings, you can have secrets. In fact, the ability to keep personal, private thoughts secret, without feeling as though you are deceiving, signals that you have developed healthy boundaries. You don't need to tell anyone your entire relationship, or sexual history, unless you want to. Of course, if you have a sexual disease, you have a moral obligation to share this information with a potential sex partner before having sex. This right to privacy does not include any type of deception, such as hiding extramarital affairs. Deception causes harm to others. What it does include is a personal right to keep your secrets tucked away behind your boundaries. Your secrets belong to you; they are yours alone, as long as they are not harmful to others.

Maintaining and Protecting Your Boundaries

Your boundaries have another benefit, as well: they give you the opportunity to teach your partner who you are. Because everyone has different values and priorities, everyone's boundaries are different. My boundary may

133

be; "I won't accept people being late when they have an appointment with me." Your boundary, on the other hand, may be: "As long as you show up within a half hour of when I expect you, being late is no big deal."

You tell your partner what you like and don't like, and what you consider acceptable and unacceptable behavior. In teaching your partner about your limits, you are automatically setting boundaries for the behavior you can expect from your partner later on. And, as you communicate your boundaries, you are demonstrating your own behavior.

Once your boundaries are established and under-stood, your partner knows that invading them without your permission will yield predictable consequences. Your partner knows this because you taught him the rules ahead of time. If more couples shared this vital information with one another, many relationship prob-lems would be avoided.

Because your partner knows your limits and bound-aries, he or she can opt to ask your permission to cross them, and, because you are the gate-keeper of your boundaries, you can choose whether or not to grant such permission.

It's acceptable for your partner to cross your bound-ary if your partner first asks for permission, and you grant permission. When they began to date, Julie taught Mark her boundaries around her family. "We are an extremely close-knit family," she explained to me in a counseling session, "and I told Mark that I always spend Sundays at home with them. It's very important for me to spend time with my parents and my brother, and I thought Mark needed to know this. All of my past boyfriends complained about how much time I spend with my folks, but it's important to me."

134

Mark respected Julie's boundary and never attempted to manipulate her into spending Sunday with him. If he wanted to be with Julie on a Sunday, he'd either go with her or try to negotiate an alternative acceptable to both.

Once in a while, though, a special event held on a Sunday—a concert or sporting event—would attract Mark's attention. He would ask Julie whether or not she wanted to accompany him to the event. He would ask her, in other words, for permission to cross her boundary. Mark didn't complain, bully, or use guilt to get his way. As a result, Julie felt she had the breathing room to decide about whether or not to join Mark. Most of the time, she agreed to go with him happily.

Julie and Mark's sharing of, respect for, and asking permission to cross each other's boundaries made the relationship harmonious. Julie's wants were validated. She expected nothing less than complete respect for her boundaries from Mark—and she got it.

It feels good when your boundaries are remembered and honored. Your partner shows this by asking for permission to cross them.

Frank shared his boundary with Michelle early in their marriage. "I want to sleep in on my days off from work," he told Michelle, "and I'd appreciate your allowing me to sleep as long as I need to."

Michelle honors Frank's boundary, and she leaves the house to do errands on Saturday mornings. She keeps busy, and has a productive morning, and Frank gets to sleep in a quiet house.

On those Saturdays when she'd like Frank to accompany her, she asks him ahead of time. Frank is then free to choose whether to get up early, or sleep in.

Couple Boundaries

When two people are in a relationship, boundary overlap is inevitable. The partners' boundaries can be complementary—for example, both partners wanting to watch the eleven o'clock news each evening. Or, they can be dissimilar—for example, one partner wants children and the other partner wants to remain childless. Such a collision would require negotiation, so that one partner won't feel violated

There are many areas in which boundaries can cross within a partnership:

> decisions about how to spend free time
> decisions about spending money
> decisions about saving money
> decisions about career changes
> decisions about where to live
> decisions about having children
> decisions about how to raise children
> decisions about where and how to celebrate holidays.
> decisions about friends and social issues

In the beginning of a relationship, unhealthy people have strong need to feel their new love shares a lot in common with them. It is a way of feeling fusion with a partner, a product of an incomplete individuation-separation process.

Consequently, they are reluctant to share their boundaries with their partner. They may even blind themselves to their partner having boundaries different from their own, thus preserving the illusion of fusion.

It is inescapable: all couples have individual—as

well as joint or overlapping—boundaries. Boundaries are healthy; sharing them with your partner preserves—rather than threatens—the bond between you. When your partner sets a boundary, it isn't a rejection of you. By sharing a true boundary, as opposed to a wall, your partner is showing self-respect. Your partner is saying, "I want you to know me, and how I want to be treated." A boundary is a map of one's personal territory, sharing it with you is a complimentary statement about your partner's feelings toward you.

The sandbox

It's helpful to think of a couple's boundaries as a sandbox. I get this analogy from having two cats at home. Although both cats share one sandbox, each is responsible for covering his own "stuff." When each cat takes responsibility for his own stuff, everyone benefits. But when one cat leaves his stuff uncovered, and then expects the other to take care of it, a smelly, messy box results.

In a relationship, we have a similar mess on our hands when we expect our partner to take care of our responsibilities. In a healthy relationship, both partners know what their stuff is. This division of responsibility is decided and understood through communication and negotiation.

The communal sandbox is a boundary around the couple. It represents issues that together affect the couple. These issues can involve money, time, housing, careers, taxes, child care, religious practices, medical help—anything that jointly affects both partners.

Occasionally, the communal sandbox can involve a people outside of the relationship. In such cases, the couple needs to act as a unit when negotiating with these other people, to ensure that the couple's collective wants and needs are met.

For instance, when their next-door neighbor drops-in unannounced during their peaceful dinner hours, Stan and Marta worked together to set a communal boundary. "We both told our neighbor that she was welcome to come over, but that she needed to call first," said Marta. "We also told her that we ate dinner around half past six, and we would appreciate her respecting our schedule."

Taking care of mutual wants is part of being a fulfilled couple, in the same way that taking responsibility for individual wants raises your self-esteem. Both partners work together to ensure that the couple's mutual wants are met.

11

RED FLAGS

Many of my clients enter therapy complaining that their spouse has changed since they were married.

"He flirts with other women," a wife complains.

"My wife doesn't appreciate all the things I do for her," a husband says.

In reality, these characteristics were there from the beginning. In fact, red flags signal potential problems from the first date forward, but those signals were ignored.

Your mate didn't develop irritating or unacceptable behavior overnight. You chose not to acknowledge the behavior when you first saw it. You kept blinders on, not wanting to burst the bubble of perfect love.

Perfect love, as the media portrays it, is much different than healthy and functional love, as I define it. In romantic novels and movies, disagreements are handled in dysfunctional ways. The heroine and the hero have a conflict. They fight, they scream, they break up. Then, they ache for one another and reunite passionately in the bedroom. Everyone sighs, "Isn't that romantic? Look how much they love each other!"

These portrayals of love running hot and cold mess up our expectations of our own love lives. When disagreements occur in our relationships, we get confused. We worry, "Does my mate's and my disagreeing mean that we shouldn't be together? Should we break up?"

The functional couple realizes that healthy love, romance, and satisfaction stem from the way disagreements are handled. Disagreements are inevitable. People disagree because no two are totally alike.

Yet, in the early stages of love, some people want to believe that their new love partner is a twin version of themselves. Often, couples newly in love can be heard to say: "We have so much in common. We see eye to eye on everything."

Please don't misunderstand me. It's important to choose mates with values similar or complementary to your own. It's unrealistic to look for a partner who will never disagree with you. It simply won't happen.

It is realistic, however, to look for a partner who will negotiate disagreements with you. Below are questions for anyone wondering whether or not their relationship is incompatible.

1. Is my partner willing to negotiate with me to fulfill my wants?
2. When I express dissatisfaction to my partner, is there a willingness to listen, and discuss the issue?
3. Does my partner respect my boundaries?
4. Does my partner keep promises?
5. Do we resolve disagreements by finding win-win

solutions, rather than win-lose conclusions (a sign of incompatibility)?

A relationship is compatible as long as three conditions are present:

1. You communicate your inevitable disagreements and your boundaries to your partner.
2. Your partner willingly negotiates those disagreements with you.
3. You and your partner honor your agreed-upon, win-win solutions.

Anything less clearly demonstrates incompatibility.

A Clear Vision

From the moment of your first date, you have opportunities to learn about your partner's character, habits, and manner of behavior. Sometimes, we don't want to acknowledge anything negative in the beginning of a relationship. We don't want to spoil the romance by seeing anything bad in our prospective love partner.

We also concentrate more on ourselves than on the new person sitting across the restaurant table from us. Oftentimes, we worry, "Does my date like me?" rather than consider the more important question, "Do I like my date?"

We are so engrossed in who we are that we sometimes assume other people are just like us. Although intellectually we know that everyone's different, our actions belie this knowledge. And when we see that our partner is different than we are, it seems unromantic, a betrayal of sorts.

The first one to three months of a new relationship are clouded by chemistry and infatuation. Our feelings of euphoria overwhelm us. We can't see through the fluffy mist of new love; we can't see that our partner is anything less than perfect. We avoid exposing our true selves to our new partners, and for our lack of candor and courage, we later pay a price.

The first few dates of a new relationship provide an opportunity to teach your partner about you, and for you to learn about your partner. Learning about one another is necessary for a healthy relationship to develop. Feigning your true feelings and beliefs during the early stages results only in failed expectations.

When negatives begin to appear in a new relationship, another opportunity for compatibility testing arises. As we've already discussed, disagreements and differences will eventually surface between any two people. The question of compatibility is answered in how those differences are handled. If the couple is willing to negotiate, a long-term, satisfying relationship is possible. If not, the couple is incompatible. Intimacy will exist only when both partners feel free and safe to trust. Intimacy is never possible when one or both partners can't, or won't, negotiate.

Good relationships are a lot of work. But continually breaking up and beginning new relationships is even more difficult. Rather than disposing of relationships over and over, in an endless pattern of serial monogamy, why not negotiate solutions with your present partner? A perpetual succession of breakups is appealing only to the phobic personality, who incites negative behavior intended to sabotage the relationship. Despite their protest to the contrary, the goal of these people is to avoid relationships and, thus, avoid confronting their fears.

Are you willing to confront your partner with your boundaries and wants? Are you willing to listen to your partner's differences? Are you willing to negotiate solutions and then commit to honoring those agreements?

Admittedly, it takes courage to face problems head-on. As I said in the beginning of this book, many people feel overwhelmed by the prospect. They prefer, instead, to stay in their turmoil-laden cycles of constant break ups and new relationships.

If you're tired of continually starting over with a new partner, if you're tired of feeling lonely in your present relationship, why not choose the option of confronting and negotiating solutions? Why not come clean with your partner about what's troubling you, and then work toward a resolution?

Spotting the Flags

"My husband, Matt, is driving me crazy!" said thirty-eight-year-old Katherine. "He's so immature and unreliable, I can never, ever count on him. If I leave anything important up to Matt, like paying bills or having the cars serviced, it will never get done. I have to do *everything* myself!"

Katherine was describing her five year marriage as though Matt had suddenly become irresponsible. Yet, when I asked her to tell me about her early dating experiences, it was clear that Matt showed his true colors to Katherine from the start.

Below are some of the early clues, or red flags, about Matt's character traits Katherine didn't acknowledge.

143

- He canceled dates at the last minute.
- He was usually twenty to forty minutes late for their dates.
- When paying for dinner, his credit card was often rejected because of insufficient credit or overdue payments.
- He didn't plan dates ahead of time; instead he'd arrive at Katherine's house and ask, "What are we doing tonight?"

During those early dates, Katherine had the opportunity to teach Matt about her boundaries. She could have told him, "When you are late to pick me up, I feel unappreciated. I will not tolerate you being more than ten minutes late. And if you're late for our next date, I won't be available to go out with you."

But Katherine hadn't allowed herself to acknowledge Matt's sloppy behavior. She had wanted desperately to view him as her perfect prince charming. If she had admitted that he was irresponsible, her romantic bubble would have burst.

Ironically, when red flags are not acknowledged, the relationship eventually falls apart. The negative behaviors always come to the surface. The partners run out of patience and say, "Enough! I'm out of here!" or they stay and become the Victim/Martyr.

It is much more effective to catch the red flags in the beginning!

By not confronting his behavior, Katherine taught Matt his behavior was acceptable. What's more, she actually enabled his irresponsibility by allowing him to be late and making all of the decisions about what they'd do on their dates. Katherine paid for the dinners when Matt's credit card was rejected. She made excuses for their late arrivals at dinner parties. She pretended not to be upset when Matt canceled their dates at the last moment. She listened to his excuses, nodding acceptance, and, thus approval. Her silence screamed: "I approve of your behavior."

In other words, Katherine was just as responsible for creating an unfulfilling relationship as Matt was.

Style versus Behavior

Everyone has ongoing behavioral characteristics that remain consistent throughout their lives. Yes, people do stop bad habits, but that only occurs when they want it to. An extremely traumatic incident, such as a change in health or the onset of drug usage, or a dramatic change in self-esteem will alter someone's behavior. For the most part, however, our collection of behaviors—our personality—remains fairly constant.

Someone who seems stubborn (or tenacious) in childhood will likely still be that way at age sixty-five. An excitable, nervous child will probably be an energetic or tense adult. The easy-going kid will become a relaxed grown-up.

These personality traits are known as your style or your mode of behaving. Do you recognize yourself or your partner in any of these styles?

>   natural-born leader
>   reserved, or shy
>   boisterous and bubbly
>   serious and studious
>   energetic
>   laid-back

curious and inquisitive
melodramatic
introspective and analytical
emotional
calm
introverted
extroverted

Styles are neither right nor wrong, they just are. Two people in a relationship do not need to have the same style in order to be compatible. In fact, two different styles can complement one another.

If a husband, for example, is laid-back, and his wife is slightly hyper, the two styles complement each other. The husband has a calming effect on his wife, and the wife has an energizing effect on her husband. She finds him soothing and comforting; he finds her exciting and entertaining. They are great together!

Styles are inborn, almost hereditary; in general, they never change. Your style is the way you are, including your energy levels and your serious or light-hearted nature. You can't change a laid-back man into an energetic go-getter. Nor can you expect a high-strung woman to be content to stay in one place. People's styles don't change.

Something that can be changed, however, is our behavior. These are the actions we carry out, such as:

the words we choose to say
the way we communicate: being hostile or being loving
the way we treat other people
the way we manage our money and obligations
the way we handle our responsibilities

146

the way we demonstrate our credibility — are our actions consistent with our words? Do we walk our talk?

Two men, with identical styles, can exhibit very different behavior. For example, Ted and Richard could both be described as driven, goal-oriented men. Their style is energetic. Yet Ted's behavior toward his wife is very attentive and considerate: he keeps his promises. He calls when he'll be late. He remembers their anniversary.

Richard, who is just as energetic as Ted, behaves much differently: Richard brings dinner guests home without warning or asking his wife. He screams abusive names at her. He writes checks from their joint bank account without recording the amount of his purchase.

The energetic style of Richard and Ted is neither right nor wrong, and, it is not likely to change. Richard's wife would be well advised to confront his unacceptable behavior and negotiate some changes.

Red, green, and yellow flags

When we first meet someone, there are clues or flags that teach us about the other person's style and behavioral habits. There are green, yellow, and red flags, like the colors on traffic signals. These behavioral signals tell a lot about the other person, and signal whether we should continue, use caution, or stop the relationship.

Green flags are positive signs: your partner follows through on promises, for example. Yellow flags signal caution, warning you that your partner's present behavior—for instance, flirting with others—could mean trouble in the future. Red flags signal serious behavior you can't or won't tolerate, such as dishonesty.

By noticing flags, we reduce or stop our illusion of being responsible for another's behavior. We cannot control, nor should we accept responsibility for, the behavior of others. This realization eliminates power struggles, as well as futile attempts to change our partner. Instead, we have three choices when our partner behaves unacceptably:

1. ignore the behavior and allow resentment and anger to build
2. confront the behavior and negotiate solutions, showing our partner how we want to be treated
3. leave the relationship

Because the third choice can be emotionally painful, it's important to spot red flags early in relationships, thus avoiding similar mistakes in the future.

You shouldn't look for the worst in your partner, necessarily, but you do need to pay attention to warning signals. For example, there are common red flags that signal potential problems. These flags are typically displayed by people who are needy, dependent, or controlling. Among those to be especially wary of:

- different value systems
- irresponsibility
- immoral or illegal actions
- disrespect for the opposite sex
- offensive, abusive, and critical language
- displays of rage
- problems-solving through conflict, win-lose solutions.
- a need to control
- instantly seductive

148

- a lack of provider skills: constant unemployment, borrows money from you,
- unable to meet financial obligations.

When Situations Change

Dysfunctional couples who have not learned to confront and negotiate problems often express resentment through passive-aggressive behavior. "I'm going to show you I'm angry at you," is the underlying thought. For example, a woman who has allowed resentment to build up during the years of her marriage may suddenly decide to stop having sex with her husband. A man who has not discussed his anger with his wife may suddenly grow a beard, knowing that she loathes facial hair.

These dysfunctional partners are attempting to punish one another. "She's changed," the man may complain. "She used to want sex, but now she won't let me touch her." She really hasn't changed, however, she never openly discussed her issues with her husband in the past, and she continues that same mode of relating today.

Rose complained that her husband, Eddie, had changed since they were married. "When we were dating, we both decided we'd have children as soon as I graduated from college," she explained. "I've been out of school for two months now, but Eddie says he's changed his mind about having kids."

Rose wanted children. Eddie said he wasn't ready for the responsibility, and he wanted to be free to travel. "It's not fair, Eddie," Rose told him during their counseling session, "you've changed on me."

I asked the couple to tell me about their earlier discussions about having children. In listening to both partners, it was clear that Eddie had always been reticent about having children. He'd gone along with Rose's enthusiasm about the kids they would have someday, figuring he'd tell her later that he didn't want to be a father. Rose had misinterpreted Eddie's silence.

Both partners had ignored important red flags early in their relationship.

Rose had wanted to believe that Eddie was equally enthusiastic about having a family. She had ignored the way he'd change the subject whenever she talked about future children. She had continually downplayed Eddie's description of children—namely, that they are "irritating, little pains in the neck." She'd also overlooked his never wanting to be with her when her young cousins were around. These were all important clues to Eddie's true feelings about children.

Eddie had wanted to believe that Rose wasn't really that intent on having children. He had held the belief: "If Rose really loves me, she'll go along with whatever I want." Eddie had also ignored important flags that would have warned him how committed Rose was to having children: He had ignored Rose's subscription to a parenting magazine. He'd minimized her picked out names for their children. And he had also downplayed her stopping to talk to every child they met.

Now that they had ignored the red flags and had gotten married, however, how would they resolve their differences? First, they had to confront the issues, beginning with being honest with themselves. Rose needed to clarify her thoughts and feelings concerning having a family. She needed to ask herself the following questions:

- Can I accept a child-free marriage?
- How important is this want to me?
- If Eddie won't agree to have children, do I need to leave the relationship?
- Are other possible solutions acceptable to me?

Eddie also needed to be clear about his feelings and thoughts. He needed to ask himself:

- How do I feel about having a child?
- How do I feel about time constraints?
- How would I feel if I agreed to have a child, or children, with Rose?
- Do I know, for certain, that Rose would be satisfied with having just one child? Or would she insist we have more?
- Am I prepared to undertake the emotional and financial responsibilities of parenthood, for my entire lifetime?
- If Rose decides to end the relationship because of my decision, am I prepared to deal with the consequences?

I worked with the couple as they confronted this issue with one another. Rose told Eddie that she valued their relationship, but knew that she'd feel unfulfilled if she never had children. Eddie told Rose that, although he might change his mind in the future, he wasn't ready for fatherhood right then.

The couple then negotiated some possible solutions:

- continuing their counseling as they examined this issue further (They were trying to put the Should we have a family? question on the back burner again. I told them they couldn't bury this issue any longer and at the same time expect to find fulfillment.)
- agreeing to have one child within the next five years
- separating, and continuing their therapy separately

Rose and Eddie finally had to face something they'd been trying to avoid: they were incompatible.

The issue of children was so vital, so important to each person, that neither was open to negotiating a solution. Rose knew she'd never be happy without having children. Eddie knew he'd never be happy with children. He further pointed out that if he gave in and had children with Rose they'd be at high risk for a divorce. And because Eddie had painful memories of his own parents' divorce when he was young, he refused to put his own child through the same heartbreak. For Eddie, having children was not an option.

I worked with them to come to terms with their decision to begin separate lives: Rose as a single parent, or with a man who wanted a family, Eddie as a single man, or with a childless woman. When a relationship dissolves, it's never easy. But it's also important not to look at it as a failure.

People usually don't come into relationship counseling with the intention of getting a divorce. It's not always possible, or advisable, to keep a marriage together. My job—as with any responsible therapist—is to help partners become responsible for to themselves. Ideally, they will negotiate their wants within the marriage. Once in a while, however, people like Eddie and Rose decide on their own that it is impossible to negotiate a solution. When the issue facing a couple involves an extremely important, conflicting, and, non-negotiable want, that is the definition of incompatible.

Me Again

The realization that a relationship is not salvageable is never easy. Guilt, anger, and loneliness are often mixed with feelings of relief and freedom. However, being single can inspire personal growth.

Being alone is a healthy experience, since you are forced to take care of your own needs and wants. It also affords time to assess what you really want in a relationship. Many people fear being alone, but there is a big difference between being alone and being lonely.

Before getting into a new relationship, it's healthy to ask yourself these questions: Why do I want to date or be in a relationship? Am I ready for a relationship? Do I understand how and why I was responsible for my unhealthy relationship patterns in the past, and my choice of partners? The answers can determine whether your new relationship will be healthy or unhealthy, satisfying or unsatisfying.

Personal fulfillment, as I've stressed throughout this book, is necessary before true love can occur. We are responsible for choosing our love partners. Self-fulfillment helps us break the toxic pattern of repeatedly choosing incompatible love partners. When we take care of fulfilling our own needs and wants, the resulting high self-esteem will inspire us to choose a new partner with care.

Preparing and being ready for a new relationship can sometimes require taking time following a breakup. At other times, it may mean getting right back on the horse. Different people deal with breaking up in different ways, such as dating on the rebound, taking time to heal after a break up, even isolating one's self.

Whatever your style, you'll be taking care of yourself by spotting red flags in new partners. There are ways to recognize red flags in other people, including asking questions about their past relationship histories, and relationship goals, plans, or expectations. If you have a non-negotiable want such as "I absolutely want to have children," or "I won't live together before marriage," communicate it before you become deeply involved. It's not necessary to tell all on the first date. Learning about each other is a process. Also, don't forget to practice good listening skills. Listen to what the other person says, not what you want to hear.

This does not mean looking for the worst in other people, or turning every date into an interrogation, just be aware, and realistic. When Jerry could only talk despairingly of the recent breakup of his marriage, Charlene spotted an obvious red flag: Jerry was not ready for a new relationship. Charlene chose to look elsewhere. By paying close attention to your date's words and accompanying gestures, you discover telltale histories, and signs of potential problems.

Acknowledging red flags early in a new relationship, before becoming involved, is an important way of taking care of yourself.

Just as you would never climb into an obviously

unsafe automobile, you should never enter into a relationship riddled with red flags; it's self-destructive. If you look for red flags, you can avoid wasting time on a painful relationship. While no love partner is absolutely perfect, being alert to red flags helps you search for someone with similar values, goals, and family history, and someone who has functional behavior.

It's so, so important to be honest and authentic from the start of a relationship. In the early stages of a relationship, many people are on their best behavior; they put on false acts and don't discuss their true feelings and opinions. Everyone wants to make a good first impression. Unfortunately, our self-consciousness makes us focus more on ourselves than on our date's potential red flags. This leads to problems and disappointments later in the relationship.

It's wise to discuss and negotiate your needs and wants early in the relationship. Tell your date what you're looking for, whether you just want a companion for movie dates, or want to get married and start a family. For example, a person who desires a long-term, committed relationship should make this known as soon as the relationship becomes serious, and always before sexual involvement. Sharing your values with a love partner is responsible, and is part of taking good care of yourself. Yes, you risk alienating a new love interest, but the greater risk is finding yourself in a serious relationship full of incompatible beliefs and goals.

Do you want to waste your time trying to change an incompatible person into a compatible partner? Do you want to be like Emily, who pretends to have no interest in marriage for fear of scaring away men? Emily is always surprised when, one or two years into the relationship, the man she's dating doesn't want to get married. "After all," the man says, "I began dating you because we both said we didn't want to get married." He meant it. She had hoped he didn't. There are many men who want to get married. Emily needs to be honest about her relationship goals so that she can attract a man with compatible goals.

When both partners understand one another's goals and values, they can negotiate as mature adults. Be honest with yourself and with your prospective partner. It's a risk worth taking. With no hidden agendas, you will communicate who you are by your actions and with your words.

Putting It All in Perspective

Taking care of one's needs and wants is part of being an emotionally mature, responsible adult. Personal fulfillment leads to fulfilling relationships, and our happiness positively affects others. We're easier to love and easier to live with when we're happy and content. In a many ways, we do everyone a favor when we take care of our needs and express our wants.

There are many options for further help and guidance, including premarital, relationship, and pre-divorce therapy. Psychotherapy, whether administered to individuals, couples, or families, is a form of higher education about one's self. If you've identified issues that need addressing within your present relationship, a licensed therapist can teach you and your partner healthy ways to negotiate solutions.

TWENTY WAYS TO RUIN A RELATIONSHIP

Why would anyone want to ruin a relationship? It's unlikely anyone tries to sour his or her love life deliberately. Yet, if you look at the behavior of some people, you'd think that's exactly what they had in mind. I can just imagine an alien from another planet observing us and wondering, "Why do Earthlings spend so much time wanting a relationship, and then, once they get in one, do everything humanly possible to mess it up?"

It's like that old joke about the woman who prayed for six weeks to find a husband. She got one, and then spent the next six years praying he'd go away. It all goes back to the question I asked previously: "What *do* you want?" If you want a fulfilling relationship, one that works, then choose to behave in a way that helps you get a fulfilling relationship. Do the things that will bring you closer to your goal, and avoid the things that move you away from it. It's actually pretty simple, isn't it? Simple, yet powerful.

In fact, there are twenty behaviors guaranteed to ruin a relationship. Some are based on common sense and courtesy; others are not so readily apparent. Those raised in loving, functional families know to avoid these behaviors, simply because their parents demonstrated healthier ways to interact. Those raised in dysfunctional families, on the other hand, did not get the benefit of early emotional education.

Below are twenty behaviors to avoid in any relationship, especially a love relationship. See if you recognize any of these behaviors in your past or present relationships:

1. *Tell your partner what to do.*
   This is probably the quickest route to turning someone off. No one likes to be controlled or directed. Phrases such as "You need to . . .," "You should . . .," "You're wrong . . ." and "you don't care about me . . ." don't sit well with people, men or women. Similarly, never saying please or thank you is also a good way to push your partner away. Never tell an adult what to do in a relationship. Instead, ask for and negotiate a change in behavior.

2. *Act as if you were your partner's child.*
   Pretend your love partner is your father or mother, and watch the dynamics of your relationship change instantly. Suddenly, you are one down in the relationship, you get to beg, pout, cry, throw tantrums, ask for permission, manipulate, threaten, or whine to get your wants fulfilled. This isn't

158

the route to feeling loved; it's the route to feeling lonely and controlled. It also makes it difficult for your partner to respect you.

3. *Act like your partner's mother or father.*
Parenting your partner creates distance and loneliness within a relationship. Unfortunately, some people confuse nurturing with parenting. The difference is this:

> Nurturing behavior is based on love and thoughtfulness. It says, I respect you and know you will meet your own needs.

> Parenting behavior is based on a desire to control, protect, and be needed. It says, I don't trust that you can take care of yourself. I will take care of you, guide you to do the right thing, and, in return, you will need me and never abandon me.

4. *Attack your partner rather than the issue.*
When your partner brings up an issue with which you disagree, how do you respond? If your partner says, for example, "I'm concerned that we're spending too much money on entertainment, and I want to discuss this with you"?— how do you respond? If you want to ruin the relationship, choose to verbally attack your partner. Say something such as, "You're a selfish scrooge! You never want to have any fun!" Such attacks are guaranteed to block communication, thwart solution finding, and create defensiveness and conflict.

If, on the other hand, you're more interested in negotiating a solution, start a discussion, for example, like, "Entertainment is very important to me, I want to make sure you're not suggesting that we stop going out." By attacking the issue, rather than the person, a win-win solution is possible.

5. *Blame your partner.*
    Point the finger at your partner for anything that bothers you, and you'll instantly relieve yourself of any responsibility, right? Of course not. The quickest route to misery is to blame your unhappiness on your partner. Blame clouds the true issue, namely:

    > The true source of unhappiness is unmet needs and wants, and boundaries that are violated without your permission.

    > You are the only person who can meet your needs, negotiate your wants, and protect your boundaries.

    > If your partner is not respecting your boundaries, you are responsible for calling attention to the problem, and then negotiating a solution. If your partner continues to violate your boundaries or act in an unacceptable manner, you are responsible for leaving the relationship.

    Blaming ruins relationships because it is an unproductive waste of time. Taking responsibility, not blaming, is the key to resolving problems. As they say: Do it once, shame on you (for doing it). Do it twice, shame on me (for allowing it).

6. *Reply before you understand what your partner said.*
Your partner is talking; you feel defensive, angry, or afraid. You are anxious to defend yourself, so you rush to reply before your partner is finished talking.

Or, your partner is talking and you really aren't paying attention to what is being said. Perhaps you're thinking of a reply rather than listening.

The result: you misunderstand what your partner is trying to say. Without fully understanding your partner's opinions and wants, it's almost impossible to negotiate. You also risk hearing something other than what your partner intended to communicate, which could lead to unnecessary conflict.

7. *Be hysterical.*
Crying, yelling, threatening—hysterical behavior is a dramatic way to get your point across, and it just may get your demands met. After all, most people hate to see their partners unhappy. Men will do just about anything to stop their wives or girlfriends from crying. Women fear the destructive, out-of-control anger of a raging man. In the long run, however, hysteria pushes people away; it creates defensiveness and blocks effective negotiation. Being hysterical is a childish way of expressing anger, and our self-esteem depends on us acting in an adult, responsible manner.

Negotiating is the adult way of getting our wants met within a relationship.

8. *Be hostile.*

You're angry and want your partner to know how strongly you feel about an issue. The issue isn't whether or not you are angry. Everyone gets angry; anger's a normal, healthy emotion. The issue is the way in which you express your anger. Acting hostile, such as name calling, accusing, and blaming, is like throwing gasoline on a fire. In a relationship, it only adds fuel to the already intense issue. Hostility, or defiant anger, is aggressive and destructive. Assertiveness, which involves staying firm about your boundaries, clearly stating your opinions and feelings, and actively participating in negotiation, is the responsible method of dealing with anger.

9. *Use demeaning words and abusive behavior.*

Abusiveness is taking anger out on a partner. It stems from low self-esteem and a desire to control others—two inherently unhealthy starting points. Abuse can be physical or psychological in nature, both types are destructive; neither should be tolerated. Both the abuse survivor and the abuser suffer from low self-esteem, and professional intervention is often necessary to break the cycle. If you are in a physically abusive relationship, either as the abuser or the abused, I urge you to get professional help immediately.

10. *Treat your partner like a possession.*

162

"My wife is a reflection of my stature and self-worth, in the eyes of other men," says thirty-three-year-old Stan. "I want her to dress and act a certain way, so I won't look bad around my friends." Stan can't understand why his wife, Bridgette, resists his attempts to control her behavior and manner of dress. "After all," he explains, "I'm just trying to improve her."

We don't own our partners. Our partners are not a reflection of who we are, although, staying with an incompatible partner does reflect a low opinion of ourselves.

Unwarranted jealousy is another aspect of possessiveness. If your partner has never violated your commitment, it's highly destructive to inflict jealousy upon your relationship. Do you suspect your partner of having an affair? There are healthy to confront such a situation, such as asking him or her directly. The unhealthy choice would be to act in a possessive, hysterical, or obsessive manner. Such behavior would erode your self-esteem and likely push your partner away.

No one wants to be thought of as an object; and we are repelled by people who treat us as such. When we think of our mates as possessions, we act and think in ways that push our partners away.

11. *Avoid eye contact while your partner is talking.*
As long as you hear every word being said, there's no need to look at your partner while he or she is talking, is there? Yes! It's unnerving to talk and not know whether or not the other per-

son is really hearing you. In addition to the lack of courtesy and respect diverted eye contact implies, is a well-grounded fear that your partner will misunderstand what you are saying. Much of communication is based on body language; if your partner isn't looking at you, he or she won't see the physical cues that reveal your true meaning.

12. *Interrupt frequently while your partner is talking.*
You know your partner well, so well, in fact, that you're able to guess what he or she is about to say. So, before your partner stops talking, you rush to reply.

This all-too-common scenario send one message: you have neither the time nor the patience to listen. An occasional interruption is certainly understandable, and even forgivable, but habitual interruption is rude, and it blocks effective communication.

What is your boundary about being interrupted? What will you tolerate, and what will you not accept? What are your partner's boundaries? Have you and your partner discussed it? If not, this might be a good starting point for you both to develop the healthy habit of negotiating and solving problems.

13. *Criticize your partner, especially in public.*
When Tamara offered her boyfriend, Ted, tips about the proper way to behave in a formal restaurant, she was being helpful. Ted felt criticized, however, feeling as though his mother telling him to get his elbows off the table. Was

164

Ted being overly sensitive? Perhaps, but people who correct their partners need to use extra caution to avoid sounding as though they are lecturing or criticizing the other person.

When your partner criticizes you, you feel like a child, with your partner as the adult; you feel inferior. Some people react to this feeling with anger, so they lash out against the critical partner. It's a common attitude: You hurt me, so I'm going to hurt you.

Every couple experiences times when one partner helps the other, or, when both partners trade information. If you offer this information without being disrespectful toward your partner, and always offer it in private, both you and your partner will feel like two adults, rather than parent and a child.

14. *Ignore your own personal hygiene.*
    A universal turn-off among both men and women is a partner who has bad body odor or who is poorly groomed. Personal hygiene is especially important during physically intimate situations, when both partners' bodies are close together.

    People who take good care of their hygiene and grooming benefit in two ways: their self-esteem increases, and their partners appreciate this symbol of care and respect.

15. *Take your stress out on your partner.*
    You've had a really bad day. Your boss was grouchy, traffic was unbearably snarled, and your mailbox is stuffed with bills. Yuck! We all

undergo stressful days, but the question is: how do we deal with that stress? Unhealthy people take their stress out on their partners. They are, in essence, kicking the dog when they're really angry with a boss, customers, or themselves.

During the drive home from work, recognize where the stress occurred (at work) and where you are going (home, where the stress did not occur). When you turn off the ignition, turn off the anger.

A functional and productive way to deal with stress is to let your partner know, you are feeling stressed out. That not only helps your partner understand your behavior, it opens the door for a cathartic discussion of the day's events. Talking about your stress can ease some of your tension, especially if you're engaged in a stress-relieving activity together; such as, taking a walk, soaking in a hot tub, bike riding, rubbing each other's feet, or lying in one another's arms.

16. *Don't tell your partner about your boundaries.*
At age forty-three, Sheila has been married and divorced three times and has lived with two other men. She estimates that she's had about fifteen relationships, none of them satisfying or lasting.

"Every one of the guys I've been with has had some major flaw," Sheila explains. "My last boyfriend wouldn't call when he was coming home late. The one before that drove recklessly when I was in the car with him. And then there was Kevin, who was a total slob around the house."

All are understandable complaints. How had Sheila conveyed her dissatisfaction to these men? "Oh, I didn't tell them their habits bothered me," she said. "I just figured it was easier to break up and start over again with a new guy. My perfect man won't have any bad habits that bug me. He's out there somewhere—I know he is."

Unfortunately, Sheila's story is all to common. She hadn't shared her boundaries with any of her partners. As a result, these men probably felt side-swiped by Sheila's sudden breakups. I can just imagine these men thinking, "Sheila never told me anything was wrong. She never told me my behavior made her unhappy. I didn't have a chance!"

The sad part is that Sheila will always feel lonely in her life and in her relationships, unless she learns to share her likes and dislikes with others. Sheila thinks she needs to wait for a partner who thinks, behaves, talks, and walks exactly as she wants him to. She believes such a person really exists, and that he will be her perfect man.

How sad. How incredibly lonely.

17. *Expect your partner to read your mind.*
   Wanting your partner to know what you are thinking, to anticipate and fulfill your wishes, to say and do the right things is an unrealistic relationship expectation. It is the product of romantic novels and movies.

   Why is clairvoyance associated with romance? It goes back to the desire to fuse, or be one with, another person—to be back in the arms of a loving parent who protects and cares for you, and who knows your wishes and wants. As infants, of course, our wants were pretty basic and easy to guess. We just wanted clean diapers, hugs, and food. If our wants as adults remained that basic, anyone could anticipate them.

But we're more complicated than that. As we mature, we each develop different interests—different standards of what we like and don't like.

We cannot expect another person to know automatically what our wants are. We must teach them.

18. *Lie, deceive, and break promises to your partner.* Trust forms a bond between two partners. When you know your partner won't hurt you, you relax and feel safe with him or her. This is called intimacy, the process of letting your guard and defenses down, and being vulnerable and authentic with another person.

Trust is a fragile condition, however. Through your actions and deeds, you teach your partner whether or not he or she can trust himself to trust you. If you keep your word, your partner will trust you. If you lie, deceive or break promises, your partner will learn to distrust you. It goes both ways, of course: if your partner deceives you, you won't trust him, or, either.

When one partner distrusts the other, or you distrust your partner, a wall is created between them. It is a barrier of protection, but also a barrier that inhibits intimacy.

19. *Have an affair.*
Gloria had been dissatisfied with her marital sex

life for years. She didn't experience orgasm with her husband, Lyle, but instead faked climax "to get the whole thing over with," she says. She believed it was futile to teach Lyle how to satisfy her sexually. And, she didn't want to explain the years of faking orgasm.

Instead, Gloria pursued extramarital affairs in her quest for sexual satisfaction. She became involved with a married coworker of Lyle's and slept with him regularly for two years. Gloria still felt dissatisfied sexually, however, because she had never taught Lyle how to please her. Since then, Gloria has had affairs with three other men, all in a vain attempt to fulfill her sexual needs.

Although Lyle has not yet discovered his wife's secret sex life, the affairs have driven a wedge between Gloria and him. They are distant from one another, physically (Gloria makes up excuses to be with her lovers, and Lyle is spending more and more time at the office.) and emotionally. (Neither partner admits how lonely and dissatisfied he or she feels.)

Affairs destroy relationships because they involve deceit. People engaged in an affair are often miserable, the result of sneaking around, lying, and worrying about being caught. Their self-esteem decreases, as well, because they know it is wrong to break a commitment. When people break a commitment, they are cheating both themselves and their partner.

A healthy love relationship requires both partners to have high regard for themselves. Both partners take responsibility for teaching one

another what they want, sexually and romanti-
cally.

20. *Discourage your partner from having any hobbies, outside interests, or friends.*
What do you do for fun? Do you enjoy sports? Or
do you prefer creative hobbies, such as, like
photography or painting? Do you enjoy taking
classes that enhance your knowledge? Perhaps
you like to dance, go to comedy clubs, or watch
foreign films.

It's important for relationship partners to maintain their own individual interests. The need for
fun and personal growth doesn't stop when we
put wedding bands on our fingers.

Both partners in a healthy relationship take
responsibility for negotiating their her own wants
for pleasure, recreation, and personal growth.
Healthy partners support one another's desires to
have fun and learn new interests. The result: the
entire relationship is enhanced, each partner
feels alive, stimulated, and excited about life.
There is more to talk about with each other,
more novel information to discuss.

Unhealthy people, who have low self-confidence and dependency issues, sometimes feel
threatened when their partners seek recreation
outside the relationship.

"What if she meets someone else, and leaves
me for that other person?" Kent worried when
his girlfriend, Trina, told him about the volleyball
team she'd just joined.

On the nights of her team practice, Kent would
use subversive tactics to discourage Trina from

attending. He'd offer to take her to dinner and a movie, or on a shopping spree. If that didn't work, Kent would use ploys to guilt her into staying, such as, "Well I guess I'll be okay sitting home all alone tonight." Once in a while, he'd even throw in a snide remark about going out to a singles bar.

Trina was healthy enough to see through Kent's actions. She confronted his behavior and the couple argued the issue. Kent learned about Trina's wants and learned that a partner's separate interest is a sign of health and growth, not rejection. The process reinforced the equality each partner must enjoy in order to have a healthy relationship. In the end, Kent developed his own outside interests, Trina felt validated, and the relationship grew stronger. Each learned the importance of taking care of themselves.

Twenty Behaviors That Ruin Relationships

1. Tell your partner what to do.

2. Act like your partner's child.

3. Act as if you were your partner's parent.

4. Attack the partner rather than the issue.

5. Blame your partner.

6. Reply before you understand what was said.

7. Be hysterical.

8. Be hostile.

9. Use demeaning words and abusive behavior.

10. Treat your partner as a possession.

11. Avoid eye contact while your partner is talking.

12. Interrupt frequently while your partner is talking.

13. Criticize your partner, especially in public.

14. Ignore your own personal hygiene.

15. Take your stress out on your partner.

16. Don't tell your partner about your boundaries.

17. Expect your partner to read your mind.

18. Lie, deceive, and break promises to your partner.

19. Have an affair.

20. Discourage your partner from having any hobbies, outside interests, or friends.

Twenty Behaviors That Nurture Relationships

1. Tell your partner what you want.

2. Take responsibility for meeting your own needs and wants.

3. Allow your partner to be responsible for meeting his or her own needs and wants.

4. Attack the issue, not the person.

5. Take responsibility for making or negotiating necessary changes.

6. Ask questions to be certain you understood what your partner has said.

7. Stay calm.

8. Express anger respectfully.

9. Avoid abuse; consider counseling if abuse is pervasive within the relationship.

10. Respect your partner's individuality.

11. Use active listening skills.

12. Allow your partner to complete his or her thought before replying.

13. Choose a private time to communicate and negotiate.

14. Show your respect for yourself and your partner by taking care of your hygiene.

15. Confront and resolve your problems at the source.

16. Teach your partner, from the beginning of the relationship, about your limits and expectations.

17. Tell your partner what you want, and negotiate solutions.

18. Be honest and keep your promises.

19. Discuss your wants with your partner.

20. Support and encourage your partner to state and negotiate his or her own needs and wants.

A Happy Ending

Happy endings take many forms. We all want to believe that every relationship can be saved, that every couple can live happily ever after. Through my counseling practice, I've learned that such a goal is unrealistic. Many couples are simply incompatible. Dissolution isn't an option, it's the only solution. Instead of "more of us," I can only suggest "someone else."

I have a sign in my office. It says: "Life isn't a dress rehearsal, this is the real thing." You owe it to yourself to address and take care of your needs and wants. If you do, it won't matter that your previous relationships ended unhappily, or that your present relationship needs improvement. As long as you learn from your past and are willing to practice what you learn in the present, your future is filled with possibilities.

The principles presented in this book work. They are deceptively simple. But I promise you: if you learn and practice them, your life will be richer. The quality relationship that has continually eluded you is within your grasp. It's up to you.

INDEX

177